From Erin with Love

From Erin with Love

Knowledge of Life After Death

Helen M. Fisher

Swallowtail Publishing

Frankl, Viktor, *The Doctor and the Soul*, New York, Vintage Books,
(Random House), 1986, p.66.

What is Death?, Harry Scott Holland, *The Dead Are Alive*, Harold
Sherman, New York, Ballantine Books (Random House), 1981.

Colton, Ann Ree, *Watch Your Dreams* (Published by the Ann Ree
Colton Foundation of Niscience, P.O. Box 2057, Glendale, CA,
1973), p.141.

"THE WIND BENEATH MY WINGS" (Jeff Silber, Larry Henley)
@ 1982 WB GOLD MUSIC CORP. & WARNER HOUSE OF
MUSIC. All Rights Reserved. Used By Permission.

"GOODBYE" (Written by Jack Blades and Jeff Watson) @ 1985.
Used By Permission.

Library of Congress Catalog Card Number 95-70407

ISBN 0-9647652-1-7

10 9 8 7 6 5 4 3 2 1

to Ron & Lizz

and to

Erin's many friends

Acknowledgements

$\mathscr{I}$n May, 1991, my husband, Ron, and I met with psychic medium, George Anderson. We owe George a tremendous debt of gratitude and deeply appreciate his sharing of his gift with us. My gratitude also goes to Joel Martin and Patricia Romanowski who believed in George and who took the time and effort to write *We Don't Die, We Are Not Forgotten* and *Our Children Forever*.

My heartfelt thanks and love to a special friend, who is known only as Bea in this writing. Bea has helped me with my grief and with my growing awareness of an afterlife. It is important to emphasize that she has never charged me a penny for her assistance. We have become very close friends. Thank you, Bea, for being such an important part of my life.

I am grateful to the following friends and family who have not only contributed to this manuscript but who have been there with love and support: Ross Bowman, Bruce Berkowitz, Lisa Carey, Kim Church, Blake Clark, Derek Clark, Robbie Clark, Wendy Cole Clark, David Farrell, Kelly Farrell, Roni Jones, Lori Fish LaBone, Erinn Nabong, Jon Richardson, Michelle Shores, Erik Sorensen, Stacey Wagner, and those whom I have identified as Gerri, Joy, and Mary.

An extra thank you is also extended to Wendy Cole Clark for proofreading the first draft of this manuscript. I know this was not an easy task for Wendy because of her close relationship with our daughter Erin.

A very special thanks to Debbie Eason for her help, but most of all for her love and support throughout the entire process of this book coming together.

My appreciation and gratitude also goes to Quan of Quan Designs for her friendship and willingness to help.

Thanks to Neal Saunders for his patience and assistance during yet another computer snafu.

I also want to thank my wonderful neighbor, Sylvia Hodge, and her friend, Adegbola Adekunle, for helping solve a printing problem. You are a good friend, Sylvia.

My appreciation to Caroline Hodgins for introducing me to Valerie Sorensen who in turn opened many doors for me. Thank you Caroline and Valerie.

My thanks and love to my daughter, Lizz, who is not only Erin's sister but also Erin's best friend. Her encouragement and belief in my ability to accomplish what I have set out to do in writing this book has helped me more than she could ever realize. I love you, Lizz.

But the largest and most heartfelt thank you goes to my husband, Ron, who, even though he is an extremely private person, has agreed to share our experiences with the world. I know this was not, in any sense of the word, an easy decision for him. I also want to express my thanks to Ron for helping in the editing process. I love you, Ron.

What Is Death?

$\mathscr{D}$eath is nothing at all. I have only slipped away into the next room. I am I and you are you. Whatever we were to each other, that we are still. Call me by my old familiar name, speak to me in the easy way which you always used. Put no difference in your tone. Wear no forced air of solemnity or sorrow. Laugh as we always laughed at the little jokes we enjoyed together. Play, smile, think of me, pray for me. Let my name be ever the household word that it always was. Let it be spoken without effort, without the trace of a shadow on it. Life means all that it ever meant. It is the same that it ever was. There is absolutely unbroken continuity. Why should I be out of mind because I am out of sight?

I am waiting for you, for an interval, somewhere very near, just around the corner. All is well.

Harry Scott Holland
1847-1918
Canon of St. Paul's Cathedral

Preface

We cannot, after all, judge
a biography by its length,
by the number of pages in it;
we must judge by the richness
of the contents....Sometimes
the "unfinished" are among the
most beautiful symphonies.

—Viktor Frankl

This was to be Erin's book. She was diagnosed with Hodgkin's Disease in December, 1988, at age twenty while a junior at Sonoma State University. She had planned to write of her experiences in hope of helping others cope with a serious illness, but "Fate" stepped in and she did not have the chance to complete her book. Erin lost the battle on Father's Day, June 18, 1989, six weeks before her twenty-first birthday.

I am Erin's mother. It has now been over five years since that tragic day in June, a day that changed our lives forever. Even though we are very private people, I have felt compelled to put together the book that Erin did not have the opportunity to complete as I have the very strong feeling this story should be shared.

This book has been written for several reasons. First, and foremost, to complete the project Erin did not have the opportunity to finish. The second, and equally as important, is to provide help to persons who are coping with a life threatening disease and to provide some source of comfort to those who have suffered the loss of a loved one. We have discovered that death is not the end; it is a transition from one dimension to another and that contact between these dimensions is possible.

Her father and I have experienced the most terrible loss imaginable, the ultimate of losses, as it is unthinkable to realize you have outlived your child. But, for whatever reason, we have also been given the most wonderful gift of knowledge a person could ever receive, the knowledge of life after death, or I should say perhaps more appropriately, life after life. And because of this knowledge we are able to feel joy again, to smile and laugh and see the beauty that surrounds us on this magnificent planet. We are learning to live around the gigantic hole in our beings caused by the loss of our daughter. Granted, there are many moments of extreme, excruciating pain and we know these moments will always be a part of our lives, but in-between these times there is a much deeper appreciation of life and all that it signifies. Erin will always be with us; we have learned to incorporate her back into our lives, in a different way, of course, but back into our lives nevertheless.

I am unable to explain scientifically how life after death

is possible but I do know that it is a law of physics that energy cannot be destroyed. Erin had such tremendous energy. Where did it go when her body died? Hopefully, you will find the answer in this book.

I have briefly covered the months of Erin's illness because that period of time is an integral part of her story that needs to be told. Also, it will explain much of what Erin wrote in her journals. **ALL NAMES OF MEDICAL PERSONNEL HAVE BEEN CHANGED.** Some names of persons noted in Erin's journals are fictitious and are designated with an asterisk the first time they are used. Interspersed in Erin's journals are comments written by those who knew her best. This will help present a picture of this person named Erin and also to validate much of what is written in the second half of the book.

The following are Erin's preface ideas taken from her notes:

First of all let me warn you that I am not a "writer." I began writing this book when I was twenty years old but I don't claim to be a writer. I'm merely a person who wants to share my story.

During my bout with cancer I discovered that there have been a multitude of books written on the disease, however, I found none that I as a young woman with Hodgkin's Disease could relate to completely. I was an active college student in the prime of my life when I was diagnosed and, believe me, there is a big difference in having cancer when you are twenty and getting it at a more common, older age.

Having cancer and going thru' the treatments was hell. I would be lying if I said it was anything better. I hope by sharing my experiences, the humorous as well as the painful...[unfinished].

Give this book to your friends and family to read. It's the real stuff and it may help them understand your feelings and theirs more clearly.

Other than a short outline and the insertion in Chapter Two, these few paragraphs are as far as Erin had progressed on her book, but I wanted to include them. I am certain much of what is in her journals would have been part of her book, also, but they were, of course, written only for her eyes. They are included here essentially as originally written, "swear words" and all. Erin had earned the right to use them.

As a mother it has been tempting to edit but I have fought that impulse because it is necessary for Erin not to be portrayed as a saint but as the real person she was. She went through the usual turmoil of being a teenager but learned from her mistakes as she went along. With her illness Erin had to grow up fast, and did. She taught us all so very much about appreciating life in her few short years.

This is also the story of a young woman not only dealing

with the agonies of a life threatening illness, but also with an often overworked, sometimes indifferent, medical profession. She has written of her hopes and fears during her illness, including the realization that an 85% cure rate meant that 15% die. There are messages in Erin's journals that point out how very important small things such as the type of hospital gown you are given can be, or the importance of having a doctor who cares enough to pull the sheet up over your bare breasts. In essence, being treated with respect as a human being. Her journals say a great deal about the relationship between doctor and patient; I think this message needs to be heard.

This manuscript also touches in a small way the story of a young woman's obsession with a rock star and her ability to end this obsession several weeks prior to her transition to the other dimension. As I think back to that time, it seems that she was somehow tying up loose ends, perhaps putting her life in order.

Accept this writing as a gift of love from a beautiful, exuberant, young women named Erin who enjoyed life with such tremendous enthusiasm. Erin made a promise to her sister that she would let us know if there was life after death and she has kept that promise.

Erin Lynn Fisher
August 6, 1968 - June 18, 1989

Chapter One

Jon Richardson: She was just a little sprite of a thing, really. To see her walk down a pathway laughing and talking with a friend reminded me of a schoolgirl, a teenager. It would not have been out of character at all for her to hold hands with a girlfriend as they went to class. When she first started Sonoma State she was so innocent she could have been Miranda from Shakespeare's "The Tempest." I could certainly hear her saying, "Oh brave new world to have such people in it!" Or something along those lines. She left an impression of smallness. Her eyes twinkled. She was pretty without being sexy. I liked her hair short. I rarely saw her sad. She wore shorts a lot. Her eyes really did twinkle. It was a pleasure to be in her company.

This was written in the spring or summer of 1988. Erin was ill but had not as yet been diagnosed:

I'm losing my mind. What a shame. And at such a young age. I wonder what the odds are of having a happy adult life if at the tender age of nineteen I have a nervous breakdown? Slim to none is my guess. But since I am not over the edge yet there still may be hope.

I could see a psychologist. Nah. I did that when I was in high school and if I do it again my mother may have a heart attack. I remember she had tried to remain calm when I announced that I wanted to see a shrink although I knew it tore her up inside. What parent wouldn't freak out? There was no reason for me to have problems, I was the "perfect" sixteen year old: head cheerleader, a good student, lots of friends, no problems. Hah! I had them all right. Being a teenager in the eighties was no picnic—much to the disbelief of many adults—but it was not the problems of sex, drugs, alcohol, etc., that worried me to the point of seeking help.

To this day my parents haven't a clue as to why I went. I'm sure that they have tried to come up with logical reasons but they don't know the truth. Even if I explained it, they would not understand just as the psychologist didn't understand which is why I only saw him one time.

He was a nice guy though. Young and friendly and non-condescending. He treated me with respect and did not patronize me in the least.

"Erin what brings you in here today?" Dr. Johnson finally inquired after engaging in irrelevant small talk meant to relax me.

"I'm obsessed with a rock star."

Shit, why did I say that. I'm obsessed with a married man with children whose profession just happens to be that of the lead vocalist and bass player of my favorite band. God, it's him, the person, not the rock star that my passion is for. Tears welled up in my eyes. This was too embarrassing. I felt foolish. I wanted to run far away and forget that I had ever walked into his office.

Dr. Johnson, unsurprised by my statement, said, "Oh, I remember treating a girl last year—a bit younger than you—who was obsessed with a rock star. Rick Springfield. You heard of him?"

"Yum, yes, I know who Rick Springfield is."

Of course I knew who he was. Every teeny bopper around was lusting for good ol' Rick for awhile. Even me. I wrote him fan letters that of course were never answered, devotedly watched him act on the soap opera, General Hospital, and spent $$ on a ticket to a concert where there were five other groups playing who I either didn't like or hadn't heard of. Waste of money? It would've been had one of those unfamiliar bands not been Ranger. [Later known as Night Ranger.]

Lori Fish LaBone: We met in college at Sonoma State University. I had already moved in and she came to the apartment and started to move all her stuff in. You have never seen so much purple and "Night Ranger" stuff in your life. I remember one night Erin and I had been drinking and going from dorm room to dorm room and somehow we got split up. I ran into these people I didn't know and started talking to them. I introduced myself and the person said, "You must be the other 'Fish.'" And from then on we were known as the "Fishes." Erin really had this way with people remembering her.

Chapter Two

*I*n November, 1988, Erin was involved in scheduling a "Night Ranger" concert at SSU. She had worked very hard to put this event together in spite of not feeling well. At that time she was not as yet diagnosed but had been extremely tired and irritable and had been to see several different doctors, including one who told her to see a psychologist because she wasn't adequately handling the stress of being a college student. No one took Erin's complaints seriously. (Her journal covers this more fully.) At one point a problem arose regarding the school's security force who feared problems with traffic, among other things, and it seemed that all of Erin's hard work would be for nothing. She was under a great deal of stress for several days, but the problem was eventually resolved and the concert would go on as scheduled.

The following are notes Erin made for her book detailing what transpired next:

ASP [Associated Student Productions] meeting where Dave Farrell said concert was still on. Immediate tension release, shoulders relaxed, yet there was pain in shoulders. Later that night drove Robert home, stopped at Taco Bell, back of neck and shoulders very painful. Robert said I pulled muscles from being so stressed. By bedtime neck was so stiff. Woke up with huge painful lump on neck. Could hardly touch it without crying out in pain. Called Mom—it was early, before an 8:00 class I think—she said go to doctor but wasn't too concerned—thought it was weird. I laid on the couch in tears (rolling not sobbing) 'cuz it hurt so bad. At student union asked Jean, Bob, and various others if it could be swollen muscle or something. No one knew, thought it was weird, but not upset. Told me to talk to Vic the intramural sports guy—he had never heard of a neck muscle doing that (especially just from stress). He said go to P.E. Dept. and I said that I was going to health center (had been to health center almost every other day around then—PAP Smears, etc). Saw Dr. Dempsey and he didn't know what it was. Said I should see Dr. Alexander (my usual) the next day. Dr. Alexander didn't know what it was—wasn't worried. Had x-rays taken and said they showed nothing so they ruled out everything serious. Absolutely nothing serious since it didn't show on x-ray but to put my mind at ease go see a special "nose, throat, ears" doctor in Petaluma.

Upon seeing Dr. Green, Erin was assured it was probably nothing serious and that it was not cancer. She was put on an antibiotic for a week and told to come back then. Erin was also sent to a nearby hospital for a CT scan of her neck. By the end of the week it was obvious that the antibiotic had not greatly affected the enlarged area in her neck, even though it was somewhat smaller. And the results of the CT scan showed a definite problem in this area.

At the next appointment we were told that, at the far end of the spectrum, it could be cancer, and Dr. Green sent her in for another scan, this time of the chest area because there was a suspicious looking shadow at the bottom of the films taken of the neck. The scan came back negative. The doctor then scheduled a biopsy which was performed December 16, and we were given the bad news. Our lovely, vibrant Erin had Nodular Sclerosing Hodgkin's Disease.

Dr. Green told us the survival rate was as high as 95% for this type of Hodgkin's Disease, and he also commented that an oncologist would probably be a little more conservative with an estimate of survival odds. He was correct. We were later told by the oncologist that Erin had an 85% chance of survival.

While still in the recovery room Erin was told that she had cancer but her main concern was, "How are my parents?" and not concern for herself. A few hours later she was on the phone telling her friends, "I have cancer." I overheard her tell one of her advisors, who was also a very close friend, that she was relieved to find out she had cancer because she had thought she was losing her mind.

Erik Sorensen: I'm not sure how much I give in to life after death, but to say that I haven't felt Erin's presence would be a lie. Whenever I'm faced with a struggle I can feel Erin pushing me to continue and succeed. Erin really is my Higher Power and source of energy. I also feel this is because of her choosing. Erin really seemed to have a grip on my potential even more so than myself. I believed this frustrated her to no end.

The following is taken from a special diary that was given to Erin by her close friend, Kim Church, when Erin had her major surgery in January, 1989:

February 20, 1989. I'm finally writing in this book. No weird thing happened that compelled me to do it. Nothing like when I first wanted to write in it but for some weird reason didn't. Actually I think I know why I didn't. When things are floating around in your head they don't seem as final and concrete as when they're in writing. Here's what happened when I first wanted to write.

It was Friday, nine days after my big surgery. I had been doing O.K. at home and today I was starting to feel like I really needed to get out and do something. It was a beautiful day so my mom went out to pull weeds and I was to sit out there w/her. At that time I was still very slow taking a shower and getting cleaned up and it was driving me crazy because I just wanted to get outside. I was in a great mood—feisty but happy. I was ready to go. I had envisioned myself sitting on the ground in the driveway w/my dog watching my mom all morning.

Things began to go down hill because my mom brought out a chair for me to sit on. I sat in the driveway on the chair...and began to freak out silently in my head. Although the chair was there because I had just had major surgery (not because I have cancer—although they're connected). I still felt like—like—. Hmmm. I felt at that moment that, wow, I am really sick. That the neighbors were watching and talking. To sum it up I thought of my story being told as a made for TV movie. For some reason my sitting in that chair reminded me of a made for TV movie called *The Charlie Wedemeyer Story* about the San Jose high school football coach w/Lou Gehrig's Disease. (I had seen that movie before I had my bone marrow test.) Of course I was still on pain medication so I think that contributed a lot to my weird thinking. Before I even went out there I had felt "drunk." Now my mind was racing, racing.

I told my mom to put the chair in the garage. I sat on the steps now. Happier but still thinking too much. My head was getting all messed up and fuzzy. Conversations with doctors started flashing in my mind: "the cure rate for Hodgkin's Disease is 80-85%." What about the other 15%? 15% die. Fuck.

Up until this time that fact had not registered *at all* with me. I kept saying over and over before this, "I'm not afraid that I'm going to die—I *know* I'm *not* going to die." I was totally serious, too. I wasn't just saying it to show I was strong or to make people feel better. I said it because I believed it (and I still do!)

but it was outside on that Friday that I realized that I could die because people have. I realized that I have a *life threatening* disease.

This was when I was having a lot of problems w/bowel movements—it was hard for me to get them out. Anyway, after being outside I went in and my mom didn't know anything was wrong. Although I did tell her this was going to be the last day of the pain medication. Switch to Tylenol.

So now I'm inside, still thinking too much. I'm getting real depressed now and my stomach is starting to get quite an anxious feeling. I went to the upstairs room and flipped on the TV. My mom checked in on me and now knew something was wrong. Then I had to go to the bathroom. #2. I went in and just sat and tried to go and that's when I lost it. I have never cried like this before. It was a deep painful cry—I felt so cold and alone but most of all I was frightened. I have never had such a horrible feeling in all my life. I was so scared about my realization that I had a life threatening disease. I was so scared about dying and I was scared about living with this agony that I felt at that moment. I sat shivering and sobbing, w/my pants down, on the toilet—trying to muffle my wails for I could hear my mother close by. Words cannot describe the fear I felt. I have never been so scared in all my life. I'm too tired right now to go on but when I start again go w/that night.

(My mom thought it was because it hurt when I tried to shit or because I was sick of having to shit—that's why she thought I'd been crying.)

Late in December we met with Dr. Maxine Nichols, one of the two oncologists who would be working with Erin. She scheduled a bone marrow test, lower body CT scan, lymphangiogram (done at Stanford) and referred Erin to a surgeon, Dr. White. Erin underwent a laparotomy (spleen removal for biopsy, plus liver and lymph node biopsies) on January 19, 1989. Results, negative, the disease was localized in the neck. I remember having to slip into the bathroom to cry after the surgeon told us the results of the biopsies. I was so relieved; it was localized and would be easy to treat.

On January 23, I received a call at the hospital from Dr. Nichols and what she had to tell me was devastating. She said a mistake had been made in the reading of the CT scan of Erin's chest taken back in November. Erin also had cancer in the lymph nodes in her chest. We were later told by the radiation oncologist at UCSF that it was not subtle in the least, the films should not have been misread. Erin's disease was now considered to be Stage II-B, the disease being in two areas, accompanied by night sweats and itching.

Roni Jones: Fish had been so brave throughout the search for the nature of her illness. She would call with periodic updates about what it was not. With each elimination of one disease or another, her hopes seemed to be high that it would be something simple. Finally, after much doubt and anticipation, we were all informed that she indeed had cancer. But, always optimistic, she told all of us that the cure rate was high and things looked good. I don't think she ever wanted us to spend our time worrying. Time is too precious to be spent worrying. In

*her eyes, we were to spend it living, because that is exactly
what she was going to do.*

5-23-89. I must say this is such a beautiful book. I
mean it. This was such a special present that Kim
gave me. Of course I'm feeling guilty because I
haven't been writing in it. I've been writing in a purple notebook of all things. I also feel bad because the
stuff I have written in here is so sloppy! This book is
too pretty for that mess!! I really mean that. Right
now I'm just in awe of this book. One of those
moods, I guess. I've decided that I want to continue
where I left off on the previous page. That horrible
day and the night that followed were the most frightening but possibly the most monumental moments
of my life. Well, I explained about that day already—
but in no way did I truly convey the way I felt. The
fear was so intense like nothing I've ever experienced again—thank goodness for that. That day on
the toilet I had worried about never being able to
shake that feeling, that panic and aloneness and pure
fear—but I did. I've never felt that again. Many,
many other feelings, that is for sure, but not like that.

That night I had a dream. But I'm not sure that
dream is the right word for it. It turned into a nightmare but not until I wake up. Strange I know but I'll
try to explain. All I remember is that in the dream
someone or something was chasing me and trying to
kill me. I don't remember what the person or thing
looked like or if I ever even saw it in the dream. The
dream seemed to go on for a long time with me just
trying to get away from this "thing" that wanted to
kill me. Funny thing is I don't remember being that
scared during the dream. I can't explain it. But any-

way the weird stuff happens when I wake up.

I wake up not too upset. But for some reason after lying there a minute or two (not hysterical or anything—just lying there), I decide to call my mom. Now this part is kind of fuzzy. I'm not quite sure if I originally called her because I was in pain from my surgery (I couldn't move too well yet and sleeping was a bitch—Mom had to help me to bed every night) or because of the dream. Whatever the reason I called out for her....calmly. That's the weird part. I was saying "Mom, Mom." Irritation. "MOM." It started off calm but when she didn't come in something snapped.

(My palms are sweating as I write this because it is so emotional to remember it.) Suddenly, I was completely terrified by the dream that I had had. All of a sudden it was like I had *just* awakened from it and had a natural reaction of terror. But I hadn't just awakened from it and when I had, I was calm. I kept calling for Mom and Dad and still they didn't hear me.

God, I'm crying right now because I remember how terrified I was and it just kept getting worse.

I started crying and screaming for them and finally they came racing out of their room. Although Mom tells me later that it was Dad that first heard me and just about broke his neck trying to get to me it was Mom that came first into the room to find me absolutely hysterical. My breathing was heavy, I was sobbing and screaming and my legs were kicking and kicking like I was trying to run away.

When Dad ran into the room the split second after Mom I was startled or something because I had to reassure myself by saying, "There's Dad, there's

Dad." I don't know why I said that. I was so terrified, so scared now of that dream. I didn't calm down at all when they came in, I just got more out of control.

They had turned the lights on and were trying and trying to tell me it was okay. I don't even know how long it took me to tell them that it was a nightmare that scared me, (I'm sure they guessed) but when I did I was just sobbing and screaming, "Something was trying to kill me." My body was just thrashing around I was so scared—it just kept building and building. I just couldn't calm down. My parents looked horrified and they later told me that they have never in my life seen me as absolutely terrified as I was that night.

They finally got me to the point where I wasn't thrashing, sobbing and screaming but I was shaking like a leaf and was completely terrified to be left alone. I did not want to go back to sleep. No way. Mom offered to sleep in the bed with me but I didn't even want to sleep that way. I was really scared. And with good reason. There was no where to hide from the thing that wanted to kill me. I realized that the day before in a way.

That horrible thing in the dream that kept chasing me, determined to kill me was my cancer. No wonder I was so afraid. My body and mind had finally figured out what the hell was happening to it and the potential danger to my *life*. I can't even begin to describe the feelings that I had because they were so deep, painful, intense. So scary.

That night my mom did end up sleeping in the bed with me but it didn't help. I didn't sleep at all. I was too scared all night. I think around 5 o'clock or something she went back to her bed but brought

Bridget up to be with me. I sat there still scared to death with the lights on and the dog digging and rolling around playfully on the carpet. I was just counting the hours until the sun would come up. This was January so it took awhile.

By this time it was daylight. I was a mess. Ten days after surgery. Someone told me the 10th day was the worst. I'm glad I had some warning.

That morning I believe I was the sickest that I have ever been in my life. Physically and mentally drained from the night. I was shaking, chilling, sweating. I had a fever—can't remember what temperature—an upset stomach—well wait. That's an understatement. I was so nauseated that I couldn't move. When the sun rose I had managed to make it downstairs onto the couch where I remained all morning. Poor Dad had to go to work but poor Mom had to stay with me. I was *so* sick. Plus my incision was a mere 10 days old so there weren't many positions that were comfortable for my sick body. And my back was in such pain, too (because of my incision and limited ability to stretch out, etc.). I think I had diarrhea that morning, too. It was hell. I honestly thought that I was going to die. That's the truth. I had *never* in my life felt that sick, was close to death I was sure of it. I remember eating dry toast. I remember it was a cloudy morning and I moved to the longer couch and Mom rubbed my legs or back or something. It helped. It calmed me down. I just wanted to go to sleep so I wouldn't have to experience the sickness anymore. I just kept shivering. God, I was really in bad shape. I fell asleep for awhile on that couch and Mom went to the store or something. I don't remember what happened that afternoon. I must've begun to feel better. But, oh what a horrible time, a horrible memory.

There's something else I'd like to write about tonight. It was late Fall '88 before I was diagnosed with cancer. I had gone thru' all the tests that summer and fall: Lyme Disease, allergies, mono, anemia, high iron content, etc. All had been negative. I had just moved back to Novato after living off campus with Lori. One day before school I was stressed and tired and I was on my way out the door but remembered that I had forgotten something in my room so I went upstairs, got whatever it was and when I came back down I was short of breath, hot and really tired.

It scared me so much because I *knew* something serious was going wrong with my health. I had known since summer. My mom walked out to my car with me—I think to help carry some stuff—and I started crying and I looked her in the eye and said, "I'm going to die, I know I'm going to die." She didn't know what was wrong with me, all the tests had been negative, but she was calm and said, "Oh, no you're not." I know she was concerned.

Just a few months ago we spoke of that day. I didn't know if she had remembered it. Boy, had she. After I had been diagnosed, she told someone at a party or something about that day. She told that person and me when telling back the story, "Do you have any idea how it feels to have your daughter look you in the eye and tell you she's dying?" It scared the shit out of her that day.

It's weird that I knew that something *serious* was wrong with me all along. Dr. Charlene Love told us during my radiation that if a patient says there's something seriously wrong she listens because a person knows. Fuck, if it wasn't for "Night Ranger" I could still be in the same scary situation. Knowing full well that I was very sick but having to put up with doctors saying, "You're doing too much. Learn to tell people 'no.' Learn to live with stress or eliminate all things that are not completely necessary in your life."

It's shit like that that makes you think you're losing your mind.

I guess it started in June, '88 when I thought I was losing my mind because I was so stressed out and could not handle responsibility. I moved into Wally World with Erinn Nabong and S. K. [They shared an apartment in a house out in the country and named it "Wally World."] I had just completed a chaotic semester at school working my ass off for ASP and barely passing classes. I needed a break. I needed summer but I wasn't going to get it. No classes but I was still working on ASP in the summer plus I had been hired for the three summer orientation programs at SSU. But that wasn't the real trouble. The Luther Burbank Center. Agh! Got a job at the Box Office and was named assistant coordinator for "Celebrate Sonoma." Having that title meant I was one of two people who were the only ones getting paid for their work on this lame program. All the other dumb fucks (and I was the youngest at 19 by about 11 years) were volunteering all their time but I was going to get $! I hated the job but I knew it would be great for my resume and I was making a lot of connections that could possibly give me a job after college. Maybe even *Sam at the LBC would see that I work there. He and Bruce Berkowitz were very close friends. Bruce really helped me get the

"Celebrate Sonoma" job and the box office. Both of which I detested. I had been working on "Celebrate Sonoma" before I started at the box office. I did most of my work at Wally World during the day. I had to call people and read this spiel to them asking for donations and shit. I hated it. I had to type them letters and shit and pick up their donations and give them comp tickets. I was really freaking out over it. I hated it. I didn't want to do any of it. I regretted every commitment that I had for the summer. All I wanted to do was sleep all day.

I was just so tired all the time. But then I started telling myself I was going psycho, trying to escape from responsibility for no reason and sleeping was an easy way out. Don't have to deal with anything when you're asleep. So that's what I started to do—a lot. I was always sleeping at Wally World but I managed to get my "Celebrate Sonoma" stuff done. I started my box office job. Worked there for one week and freaked out because I hated it and I just couldn't handle having so many different responsibilities to face (2 LBC jobs, ASP, summer orientation). I was freaking out and in the meantime really feeling shitty and run down. I was hoping that it wasn't psychological but I swear I thought it was because I was just losing it. I just could not handle any commitments. I called my mom like 3 times a day (they were living in Alameda then) and told her how awful I felt. She thought it could be allergies and she wanted me to go to Dr. Sands in Sacramento. So we both went and he checked me and then gave me a blood test for mono. He went thru' the whole stress lecture and thought maybe I was doing too much and did need a break, etc., etc. In a way this is what I wanted to hear because it was a way out. I wanted to quit every-thing. But I also wanted him to find something wrong with me for (1) then I would have a valid rea-son to quit my job and (2) it would put my mind at ease that I wasn't mentally snapping.

My mom and I were sure that I would test posi-tive to the mono. I had it when I was a junior in high school and they say you can't get it again but now there's something called chronic mono and we thought I had that. I was hoping because then I would quit my jobs. The test was negative. I didn't have mono but no one but my family knows that to this day. I told everyone that I had it. I quit my jobs at the LBC and all I did was sleep, sleep, sleep at Wally World. S. K. thought I was just depressed, "You're at a tough age, Little Erin." I was supposed to stay there all summer.

I moved back to Alameda in July. My dad never said anything but I know he was royally pissed off that I lied and quit my jobs. I was still going to make money at the summer "O" jobs but not as much as I had planned with the other two jobs.

It was at my suggestion that Erin told everyone she had mono. She was obviously ill but unless a name is given no one accepts an illness and at that time, prior to the tests results, we were certain the findings would be positive. It had to be the answer to how badly Erin was feeling. She had also gone to our doctor in Alameda for tests. All the usual blood work, thyroid tests, etc. were performed and all were negative. Dr. Sands also repeated some of these. No one thought of Hodgkin's Disease even though it commonly strikes young people. It seemed to be that if all routine tests were negative, then Erin was considered to be O.K.:

In Alameda I started to feel a little better. Low stress atmosphere helped. However, I was still going thru' tests. Back at Dr. Sands' I got allergy skin tests, a Lyme Disease test, an anemia check, and a check on my iron content. They checked that because my mom gave me a perm that turned purple when she put it on my hair—meaning that there was some kind of metal in my hair that reacted with the chemicals.

I can't even remember what that test showed. I think it was high iron in the hair but not in the blood so it didn't mean much. I think I got it in my hair at Wally World since the water stained everything orange and wasn't even drinkable. So all the tests were negative, but I was feeling better. Then the family moved to Novato. Signs of extreme fatigue showed up while I helped paint the house. I got tired beyond what would be normal for someone my age. Totally exhausted and unable to function sometimes. Like I think one time I drove my car up there before we had actually moved in and Mom and I painted all day. She probably worked harder than I did but I was unable to drive home, if I remember correctly.

We were later told by Dr. Love at UCSF that Erin had been ill for at least a year prior to diagnoses.

Erik: Erin touched me the first time we met. Her strong personal-
ity and happy-go-lucky attitude, still to this day, warm my
heart. I know Erin is looking out for me because she was the
only one who could.

In early February, Erin, Ron, and I met with Dr. Nichols to discuss treatment. I remember stressing Erin's history of allergies and how they had always affected her lungs. She had constant coughs as a child, caused by her allergies. Erin's lungs seemed to be a vulnerable area for her. I was very anxious about this and mentioned it almost every time we saw the doctors. Oddly, this was never noted on her records except by the lung specialist who attended Erin during her last week in the hospital.

Being a part of a study was discussed, the purpose of the study being to determine which form of treatment is most effective in preventing reoccurrence of the disease. The choices were total body radiation or radiation of the involved nodes followed by "mild" chemotherapy. These were both acceptable treatments for Hodgkin's Disease and not an experimental type of treatment. Erin opted to be in the study and was later chosen by computer to receive radiation and chemotherapy.

The three of us then met with Dr. Charlene Love, Radiation Oncologist, at UCSF to discuss Erin's radiation treatments. At this time Dr. Love stressed how susceptible Erin was to infection, since she had no spleen. She also wanted to really frighten us so we would not forget this critical information as time passed. Dr. Love said Erin could die within two days of an untreated infection and that she must never ignore a sore throat or fever, ever! It was interesting to us that none of the other doctors involved had given us this warning. At this time, Dr. Love also mentioned that Erin would always need to be slowly tapered off cortisone whenever it was necessary for her to take it.

Chapter Three

Jon: What took me a long time to understand was that she had a quiet ability to affect the atmosphere around her in a positive and calming way. This was so subtle that it took her absence to make it noticeable. It is an art form that will never be fully recognized because it doesn't exist in the material world but it still can affect one. Perhaps poetry is the closest kin to it. It has had the effect on me of giving my memories a kind of glow when I think of her--a feeling usually reserved for Christmas. Goethe said: "Memories are the only paradise from which man cannot be driven." Well thank God for that.

The following are Erin's notes on her six weeks of radiation therapy:

I can't even remember if our first trip was cloudy or sunny. My memory begins from the front seat of the Honda, Dad driving, Mom in back. It was so soon after my surgery that I was barely able to ride in a car—had to have the purple pillow around my belly with the seat belt over it. I remember wearing my new leather jacket and it gave me some strange sense of security. I didn't feel that then but looking back that was for some reason a predominate memory. Poor Dad gets tense driving in most places (often when he's familiar with them) but driving in the city (San Francisco) is especially hectic (to anyone who isn't used to it I suppose). We had no idea where we were going—had been given anything but helpful directions from the doctor's lovely receptionist—and trying to find a place in the city under "normal" circumstances is hard enough. My God, this family was taking their 20 year old daughter for the discussion of cancer treatment. Enough to boggle the mind slightly.

I don't remember crossing the Golden Gate or even leaving Novato. My memory starts as we began the climb up Judah Street, driving thru' the residential streets (residential for S.F. that is), muni tracks in the road, stop signs, pedestrians, looking and looking for signs to make sure we wouldn't miss it. Not much chance of that. We rose over the hill and I spotted the gloomiest most ominous set of buildings. (UCSF) They towered high above the apartment complexes, homes, churches, and Mom and Pop grocery stores that lined the rest of the neighborhoods. It was huge. Like I said, I can't remember what the weather was like before we got there but the top of that hill was surely the coldest place in all the world. The buildings were so high that sunshine or not there was a constant shade (darkness) hanging over the entire hospital and parking areas (parking areas—

now that's a joke).

The drive up Judah had been your normal "hectic drive down a street in S.F." but the minute we reached the "hospital zone" it seemed to turn into sheer craziness. It wasn't just because of our tension (although that was mounting) so it wasn't our imagination. Pedestrians were everywhere—middle of the street, sides of the streets, cracks in the streets. The road got much more narrow, some building construction site on the left, buses, policemen, doctors, sick people, food wagons, pylons, parking lot signs that said FULL. Dad, in all of this confusion, kept his head pretty clear and knew the best thing would be to drop Mom and I off at the front entrance. We would then enter this monstrous building while he searched the streets for a parking place. Mom and I figured we would never see him again.

I always thought that hospitals were supposed to be as calm, relaxing and quiet as possible. I mean—come on—this is a place for SICK PEOPLE! Well, we walked in and the atmosphere from the outside had already beaten us in. It was just as crazy inside. Maybe worse because at least outside there were more places for those pedestrians to be. Inside they just filled the halls, the waiting room, the bathrooms—ACK!! Mom and I got directions to the basement where the Radiation Oncology Department was (woman at the front desk didn't speak English too well so it's a good thing she gave us clear directions on the first try). After traveling down and down the noise filled halls—no, noise is not a strong enough word here. There was construction going on in various places—paint fumes—*loud* drills, hammering—you know things that tend to calm one's

nerves. Anyway, something really frightened us
about these hallways. On the walls they of course
had directory signs like: Admissions➜ ←Restrooms
Radiation➜ but they also had huge "murals" of
street names so you could find your way back to the
street.

Oh, my God, we really weren't going to see Dad
again! Mom and I made it down to Radiation without any problems at all (unbelievable) but once we
were there we discovered that we had to go back up
to admissions first. Nice of them to tell us to come
early for that. My appointment was at 11:00 in the
Radiation Department and at 11:00 I was in the
Radiation Department. Not for long. Back up the elevator, thru' the crowded halls, the construction, the
chaos, to admissions. Wrote my name in cursive and
thought they'd *never* be able to read it (they were for-
eign and even my name printed might be a chal-
lenge). Somehow, without any struggle, we met up
with Dad. It had taken him that long to park and just
when Mom went walking toward the front entrance
they met up. Unbelievably lucky, we saw Dad again.
He parked blocks away in a neighborhood he was
sure was home to all doctors—had to walk a *very*
steep hill and said there was no way I would be able
to do it (my surgery so recent and all).

So we waited and waited in admissions watching
all the sick people and all the people in their 49'er
clothes. They had won the Superbowl only a few

weeks ago while I was in the hospital. People were still flying high from their victory.

The people working in this busy, busy admissions office never seemed to catch on to the fact that if you move quickly and efficiently things get done, people can go to appointments, etc., etc. They moved so slowly it boggled the mind—just meandering around. We laughed about it, more than stressed about it, because it was so ridiculous. My name was finally called—correctly—and the three of us jumbled into a small cubicle to give the man and his computer the needed patient information. Very routine process but in the *middle* of it the funniest thing happened. A cleaning lady comes in loudly humming, moving very slowly, into this tiny, tiny, already cramped cubicle and with tortoise-like actions begins to dump the waste paper baskets. The guy working in there didn't even bat an eye, while my parents and I were dying to try to keep a straight face. We finally got my plastic UCSF credit card and we were on our way back down to Radiation.

The trip down the long, crowded, noisy halls wasn't as bad as the first because we knew exactly where to go. I was leading the way with a fast pace and look of confidence (it was actually pure adrenaline and fear) which was a mistake because I should not have been so anxious to get off that elevator. I was first off and rounded the corner to where my mom and I had been before. Round the corner, face to face with a man pushing a gurney with a dead guy on it! The dead guy was covered but that didn't matter. The man pushing him was obviously trying to hurry and when he saw the horrified look on my face his eyes widened and he pulled him into the "service elevator" *very* quickly. My parents rounded the corner, never saw it but came face to face with me as I abruptly turned around, white face, shaky voice, and told them I just saw a dead person. Then it really hit me and I lost it. A DEAD PERSON on the floor where I'm going to be coming for my treatment EVERYDAY. THEY'RE DOING A GREAT JOB HERE! Then I thought about Lara [a very good high school friend of Erin's who died at UCSF] and when she died and I thought how that could have been a Lara under there—not just some dead guy. The whole thing was terribly traumatic and emotional. I was trying to seek escape into a side bathroom only to discover it was locked. Jesus, I couldn't even hide to cry. I stayed in the nook off the hall for a moment and got myself together. Terrific start!

I don't remember much about waiting in the waiting room that first day except that it was much more pleasant than the rest of the hospital. There were a lot of people there but it was pretty calm. The waiting room had a child's section with stuffed animals, books, toys, table and chairs. There was a fish tank, pretty pictures on the walls, some cancer information and a big latchhook rug that read in rainbow colors: "Happiness is the last day of treatment." Hmmm. It seems like I won't be knowing that feeling for a long time. All I know is "shit is right now."

There was something else about the waiting room and that was the "basket" on the front desk. Just a little basket like the kind you put rolls in or something but it was the center point of that room. Everyone did something different with it (everyone meaning patients, the front receptionists, doctors, technicians). Some people put pink cards in it, some people took them out. Some people wrote something on blank paper—provided—and put it in. Some people would do nothing. People would come in and put things in, take things out and there was no rhyme or reason whatsoever because it wasn't consistent. It wasn't like the patients were always putting in and the doctors taking out, everybody did everything—very weird. I guess I'll be learning about that soon enough.

A very nice nurse came in to get me and my family. She was short, young, blond, cute, normal-looking and real friendly. She (Laura Bannister) asked how I was and I told her I had seen a dead body so I wasn't off to the best start. She asked if it was on this floor but didn't seem surprised when I said yes. Encouraging.

Laura put us in a room that was directly at the end of the hall where I had seen the dead body. That was O.K. though because it ended up being a funny thing (not the dead body—but the hall and the room). I think Laura did the normal examining things (I can't even remember) and then left us in there for the resident to come in for a further exam. Resident? I hope he's gorgeous and young. But wait, do I really want some med. student learning on me? I later found out the difference between residents and medical students. So anyway, we were left in this examining room with the door wide open so we could see all the action outside. Lots and lots of people passed that room. Mostly people that worked there. We found it incredibly hard to figure out who were the doctors, the nurses, the receptionists, the orderlies, the residents, etc. Most of the people that we saw (at least I felt this way and I think Mom and

Dad did too) were not people who I would want to have as my doctor. I knew I was seeing Charlene Love but I had no idea what she looked like so every female with a white coat that walked by I thought, "I hope it's not her, she looks kind of gross, she looks mean," etc. My mom had talked to her on the phone and said she was an extremely gentle woman. Let's hope so.

So anyway, we are getting pretty antsy and bored because we've been sitting in the room a long time and still no resident or doctor. We start to get kind of delirious and silly and we get caught more than once by passerbyers who see us making really silly faces. Then my dad, who is sitting on a stool with wheels, starts moving it around in a way that Mom and I are sure he is going to fall. We get sillier. Here's where the hallway comes in. The hallway had a slope and the slope led right into our open room. We thought it would be great to take turns pushing each other down the hallway ramp into the room on that fun little chair Dad had. That was it, we were in hysterics. It seems like about that time the resident came in. Female. Just my luck. Shy but nice. She didn't wear make-up, had short hair and talked real close in your face. But I excused it because she was still learning about dealing with patients. She was very nice though, although she gave me quite the exam right in front of Mom and Dad. Up until then doctors had been real careful about that, making them stay out and stuff. Not Michelle Vincent, boy. No, it wasn't that bad—and I know they were trying hard *not* to watch.

We could never figure out what nationality this woman was. Not that it mattered but she was very interesting looking. My father thought for sure she was European. I suggested Danish or Finnish. We'll never know.

We finally met Dr. Love. The resident had left and come back with her so all five of us sat in the room. Dr. Love's eyes were HUGE! That was the first thing you noticed about her—couldn't help it! HUGE..but very kind. I could tell right away that this woman cared about me. What a relief. She was extremely well groomed and dressed nicely (not the fashion statement that Maxine Nichols makes but she gave it a good shot).

As she sat on the examining table and talked of so many things I can only remember a few. We talked about the study, the different legs of it, the side effects (hair loss is one thing I remember discussing, it was only for a certain kind of radiation and it would only be about 2 inches in the back, I said no biggie and they said get a perm and let your hair grow—it was casual on both parts).

Throughout all this, the big memory is my poor father sitting on that stool in his 3-piece suit so concerned, so tense, so scared, so uncomfortable. It wasn't hard to pick up—my mom and I knew. Michelle had sensed it (we talked to her later). That memory and another, Dr. Love had to tell us something really scary that none of us was prepared to hear (it seemed to happen a lot though). When she explained that because I don't have a spleen that I could die within 2 days of an "untreated" fever or infection (sore throat for example). I thought we were all going to faint.

Funny how Dr. White who took the spleen out of my body failed to mention this rather major fact. And this, she made *very* clear, is the way it will be for the rest of my life. She said, "I want to scare all of you. You'll remember this for about 5 years but then you'll have a family and your kids will have colds and you'll get one and not do anything about it. Every year someone dies that way." Also, I always have to travel with penicillin like when I go to places where it would be hard to get in an emergency. That's some scary information to say the least.

The disease responded very fast to radiation treatment and I remember how ecstatic the resident, Michelle Vincent, and Dr. Love were after the first few treatments, and how excited Erin and I were at their enthusiasm. At this point all seemed to be under control.

Erin had devised a visualization technique she used during her radiation treatments. The good cells were little characters with Jack LaLanne bodies and Elvis Presley haircuts. She visualized them eating up the cancer cells during each of her treatments. A friend jokingly suggested that the good cells have a pet, so Erin visualized a little puff-ball type animal. She told me that in her mind these little animals immediately turned into huge furry creatures that devoured the cancer cells. On her last day of treatment, Erin informed me that she knew the cancer was gone because in her mind she could see the good cells walking peacefully in a sea of flowers.

No evidence of the disease was visible on a CT scan following her six weeks of radiation. Her treatment had been successful.

On March 27, 1989, Dr. Nichols prescribed prednisone (cortisone) prior to the above mentioned CT scan, because Erin was exhibiting signs of allergic reaction caused by the dye used with the scan. I mentioned to Dr. Nichols that Dr. Love had told us that Erin should always be tapered off cortisone. She replied, "She only means after long term usage." I was still uneasy and had Erin taper off as much as she could with the pills we had available.

Chapter Four

*M*ichelle Shores and Lisa Carey (cousins): *She was always making sure people laughed and were kept entertained. She was always glad to see you and if she knew you were coming to visit she never made plans to do anything else. Erin was always happy, cheerful and full of creative ideas.*

5-25-89. Tuesday, May 16th, my mom and I returned to UCSF for a 2 month follow up visit. The first thing I noticed was that the towering buildings of the medical center can be seen immediately when the turn on to Judah is made. They are straight ahead and up on a hill so it's strange the way I had earlier described our search for them. I wasn't "special" anymore and couldn't park in the cheap, quick and easy radiation/emergency parking lot so we had to park across the street in the big garage. The wind was blowing like crazy and of course I was wearing a hat—a beret—which was very hard to keep on.

She was wearing the hat to cover the small hair loss caused by radiation. One Sunday morning, following several radiation treatments, I remember going into Erin's bathroom and seeing her standing at the sink with big clumps of hair in her hands and really acknowledging to myself what horror was happening to her and how very serious and dangerous this treatment was. The look on her face, even though she remained calm, told me she was experiencing the same horror I was feeling. Erin wore her hair short and seemed, at least outwardly, to be able to accept the hair loss—it extended up about two inches in the back. She was concerned about a complete loss of hair when she started chemotherapy and we looked at wigs and she tried on a few but opted for hair bands and a variety of cute hats. Luckily, that fear of losing all her hair was never justified. She looked more like a model when she went out wearing her hats than a person undergoing treatment for cancer. Always a beaming smile on her face. Very few around her were aware of the inner turmoil she was experiencing:

———————————

Plus I had this damn short black mini skirt on and with my hands raised up to hold onto my hat the T-shirt I was wearing hiked up revealing an overweight girl in a too tight skirt. Enough about fashion.

It was strange to be back at this place but it wasn't that upsetting. Probably because I knew I had survived!

After climbing down the stairwell, stopping to check my hair and hat in the glass frame of a picture, we entered the hallway (yuk, that bothered me a bit) and then into the reception area. I gave the latchhook rug a knowing look, told the lady I was here and sat down and waited and waited. I read most of a very interesting article in the *San Francisco Focus* magazine about an alternative health care plan/hospital wing called Plaintree (I think that's what it was). Some lady from another country started it after she came to, I think, California and was appalled with the way hospitals operate.

The Plaintree hospital ways are very different. Patients can enjoy live music and other entertainment such as painting or something. Their families and friends play key roles in helping out and each patient always has the same nurse. Sounds great—maybe someday I'll be connected with that or something similar.

The nurse, one I had seen often during my treatments but always kind of disliked (young, blond, softly permed long hair), finally called me into an examining room. But first she stopped to weigh me. BITCH! (The black orderly was in there and then left. We didn't speak. I didn't look at him long and I don't even know if he could've recognized me—moon face and all. I'll write about this guy later.) I weighed in at an all time high that nearly sent me into hysterics, 137. Oh, my God. During radiation I was around 124-126. I turned to my mom after I got off the scale and I said, "Don't say a word." She said, "How much?" so I guess she didn't see. I didn't tell her.

So now I went in and had to put on a gown (the bitch nurse had a whole stack of gowns she could've thrown—just like my choice in the radiation dressing room everyday—and she gave me the worst, the blue and white striped silky polyester one. Agh! I got a different one the minute she left) and took off my hat which left my hair very flat and gross which emphasized my chipmunk face. I looked pretty bad.

The medical profession needs to know how important something as simple as these gowns are to patients. Erin was delighted one day when she was handed a bright purple gown:

Dr. Vincent came in first. Very relaxed now. Starting to almost be like a real doctor. Then Dr.Love came in. What a saint. She examined me and looked at that mark on my scar. She thought it looked like it could be a zit. Ooo! A zit, that's pretty gross, she wasn't concerned but told me to put hot packs on it to try to draw stuff out if it's filled up with anything. Then we just talked. First about the steroids. Now remember this was after I had my one time breathing troubles and was given steroids which cleared it up completely and I was now being tapered off. She said that the breathing problems (caused by the radiation) were probably initially brought into an active state due to the Decadron that they gave me for the short time right after my chemo treatments. Ironic, isn't it? The damn steroids brought it on and now I'm stuck taking them to keep a problem away that they started (well, I know the radiation did it but it didn't flare up until the steroids—Dr. Love's theory at least). I told her how much I hated being on them and she could see what they were doing to my appearance. She said I should never be on cortisone (the steroids) again after I taper off with this batch. It has to do with my spleen being gone. I had taken steroids before each CT scan I was having, too, to avoid problems with the iodine. She said from now on I should have either CT scans without the contrast or have MRIs. What a relief to hear that. These steroids are a drug from hell.

Then we just talked about me and basically my emotional state. She is so understanding, she seems to know exactly what I'm going thru'. I told her how I had been thinking of being ASP President next year and her jaw just dropped. She *could not* believe that thought had even crossed my mind. She told me she didn't even want me to take a full load of classes in the fall! She thinks I should just take two and concentrate on getting myself healthy. My mom interjected that people were putting pressure on me to do things like ASP and saying, do as much as you can, you need to get out, etc., etc. I added that people think I just sit around depressed but I don't. My mom also added that the people at school only see me when I feel O.K. and have make-up on, and am able to be there, and those times aren't often. But when they see me doing okay at school they think everything's fine and I'm ready to get back in action.

Dr. Love said, "Wrong. Nobody understands. They are afraid. They don't want to accept the fact that you're not okay and that it's going to take a long time for you to recover." When they see me feeling okay they are able to forget the terrifying reality of what has been going on with me and that it could easily get them, too, at anytime. They want me back around doing things so they don't have to deal with their own fear. Dr. Love also pooh-poohed the idea of doing as much as you can. She was just so concerned about me. And she says I have every right to feel shitty about what's happening to me. God, it was so nice to hear her say all that. It was just what I needed at that point because it was just the day before that I withdrew my ASP Chair application and was feeling some resentment from (and toward) people. When the Dr. was ready to leave she gave me her card and said to call anytime about *anything*—and she meant it. Then she gave me the warmest most sincere hug. I had to fight back my tears and as I looked down at my mom, I noticed she was too. How lucky I am to have this wonderful woman as one of my doctors. She requested to see me again after my last chemo treatment, mostly as an emotional crutch as I begin my new life as a recovered cancer patient back in the swing of life. She realizes that it's going to be hard to just jump back into normalcy. Thank God I'm not the only one worried about it.

Bruce Berkowitz, Advisor, Associated Student Productions: My first impressions were somewhat classic. Here was an attractive, friendly and obviously enthusiastic young woman who was transferring to SSU because Hayward State was no fun and she didn't feel connected. Erin was eager to get involved in student activities. This was too good to be true. Would she really turn out to be as wonderful as appearances would indicate? I had learned to be a bit cautious with my hopes but with Erin I had the feeling she was prime ASP material.

We talked for awhile and set up a time for her to meet the ASP crew. She immediately fit right in. She and Erinn Nabong bonded like long lost sisters. It was the beginning of a very special two years for all of us.

Everyone on ASP, including myself, had never been closer. This was a true family. And like all family, it had highs and lows, laughs and tears. But we always had love and respect. Yes, this was the beginning of something unique, something forever.

5-28-89. Getting simulated for radiation. I don't remember anything about before and after but the process took a long time and Mom and I didn't leave UCSF until it was dark (of course it was winter so it got dark early). A pretty, young hispanic woman named Megan did my simulation. She was a little rigid, could've been nicer. I had to lay on a very hard table for about two hours with my head tilted back on a neck "rest" and taped to the table. Ouch! They let me up a few times during that to stretch, but God was I sore! Most of the time the lights were off in the small room I was in and only red beams prevailed. There were signs that cautioned of radioactivity. That's always a nice feeling—to be alone in a dark room with red beams and signs like that. They did their first art work on me that day. War paint I call it. Four big purplish blue crosses to mark the field of radiation. Actually they drew more. They would paint me up and then Dr. Love would come in and want a minor change or something so they would *scrub* all the old marks off with alcohol (ouch) and paint new ones on. They had some shit on my chin at one point and the alcohol didn't exactly get it off so I was glad it was dark when we left the hospital!

The geeky oriental guy that wore too short polyester pants made his first appearance that day to take some measurements of me. He wasn't friendly at all.

Just came in, shoved ruler-type things under my back and over my *bare* chest. Yes, I was lying there with my tits exposed most of the time. Dr. Love always came in and pulled my gown back over my boobs but someone like Megan wouldn't care, just wanted to get the job done and would expose me again. (I got used to having my tits exposed having to be in that position during treatment every day for six weeks.) Mom had been in the little waiting room for the first part of my simulation but then started wandering around the hall (my room was only a few feet from where she was) and was able to stand and watch some of what they were doing—always had to leave when they took x-rays and stuff though—only radiation for the patient!

All had been going well. I was sore but this was nothing I couldn't handle. I was getting increasingly nervous however because Dr. Love had said they were going to have to give me little permanent tattoos. Little dots to help line up the radiation field. Permanent just in case in some years to come I had a reoccurrence they could see exactly where it had been lined up before. Tattoos. Ouch. This is going to hurt. Then they decided not to do the tattoos that day. Whew! But wait, maybe it would be better to get them done now and it over with so I don't build up a lot of anxiety worrying about the pain. Then for some reason they changed their minds and decided to do it. Megan was in charge. I told her to be gentle. Okay, here comes the first one. Be brave. "Tink." That was it? I barely even felt it. What a relief. Megan did the rest, even had to do one over but it was nothing. Thank goodness. I survived simulation.

Ross Bowman: Erin was a serious, thoughtful little girl, yet friendly and outgoing. I am sure she had a positive impact on all who knew her. Because of Erin I am a better person, more aware of how precious is our time here with our loved ones. Although she isn't really with us, to me she isn't really gone. She is just a little ways ahead on this road of life. Somewhere along the way Erin is waiting for her grandpa. Who knows, perhaps just around the next bend.

6-4-89. Major thing I forgot to mention was the study but I don't want to go into that right now. I'd rather talk about the other major thing—my armpits! Anything in the radiation field was not to be touched with soap, lotion, deodorant, or razors. Nothing. My right armpit was in the field so that meant no shaving, no *soaping* and no deodorant for a straight six weeks. That blew me away more than just about anything they had told me up to that point. Dr. Vincent found it especially amusing that I got so "upset" over it. (My dad's theory: She is European and doesn't shave or use deodorant!) There were many jokes made and they did say that after awhile I wouldn't need to worry about it because my armpit sweat glands would dry up and the hair would fall out and stop growing. Well that at least was a relief but until then I would just have to smell? Oh God! The one thing I could use was corn starch. Yeah, I'm a true Granola now! Everyone also said, "Well you'll have one good armpit."

Later Dr. Love decided to cheat on the study and go a little extra so she did most of the other pit, too, but didn't start until about three weeks into the radiation (if I remember correctly). Actually my first armpit was technically supposed to be avoided too (I think) as was the higher part of the back of my head but Love and Vincent "had a feeling" that they should go one lymph node over everywhere just to be sure. It was cheating on the study but she checked with the main guy, I think, and anyway she was trying to save my life. Let her cheat all she wants! Oh, and not washing also meant that those damn war paint crosses were on for six weeks. Good thing it was winter so I could wear turtlenecks. Dressing was very hard.

Kelly Farrell: "Sparkling purple socks and an "I'm a Pepper" T-shirt: My introduction to Angove's 7th grade P.E. class and Erin Fisher. Erin's personal style...made expressing yourself in wacky clothing popular.

Chapter Five

*O*n Tuesday, April 4, Erin had her first chemotherapy. Following this, she had some difficulty catching her breath. The nurse had Erin sit for approximately fifteen minutes until her breathing became normal. The doctors had left the office prior to this. I was very concerned, but the nurse did not seem to be.

The three drugs she was given were methotrexate, bleomycin and vinblastine. Methotrexate and bleomycin are both known to affect the lungs in some instances. Bleomycin is known to cause lung scarring but, it was stressed to us, scarring usually occurs only in older patients.

Following her first chemo, Erin had many side effects: fatigue, red and itchy palms, slight fever, nausea, headache, muscle pain in arms, legs and back, stinging mouth, pain in ears and jaw, pain in joints of hands, depression, stomach ache, cough and trouble breathing, chest pains, dizziness, mood swings and weakness. She was extremely lethargic and refused to eat or drink, and I was especially concerned about her shortness of breath. But when I described this to Dr. Nichols, she said, "I don't call that shortness of breath."

Dr. Nichols had called Erin following chemo to see how she was doing, and I overheard Erin saying she was okay. When I questioned her as to why she had not told the doctor how badly she felt, her reply was, "There are people so much worse off from chemo than I am. I don't want to complain." I immediately got on the phone and told the nurse just what was transpiring. (As far as I could determine, this phone call was never noted on the records, which I later requested.)

Later that week Erin was sent in for a chest x-ray because of a cough and difficulty breathing. We were told it showed no problem, and that everything was okay. She spent the entire weekend spread-eagled on her bed in extreme muscle pain. So much for mild chemotherapy.

On April 11, Erin had her second dose of chemo. I was very concerned about the breathing problem she had exhibited following her first dose of chemo the previous week and I mentioned my concerns to Dr. David Gold, Dr. Nichols' partner. He said, "What breathing problem?" Dr. Gold either had not read the records from the previous week, or the nurse had failed to make note of this occurrence. (I later discovered there was no mention of this difficulty in the records.)

Erin related the side effects from the first chemo and Dr. Gold told the nurse, "Oh, we forgot about Decadron (cortisone), we'll add it to the chemo." 10 mg. was added, to the best of my knowledge, to alleviate side effects. In a letter Dr. Gold wrote to Dr. Green, the ear, nose and throat man who had referred Erin to him, he listed her side effects and wrote, "I think she watches too much television." I am assuming he was making a joke but, believe me, I found no humor in this letter when I was perusing her records.

Dr. Gold also prescribed 16 mg. per day of Decadron for the next three days. He made no mention of tapering off the steroid. At this point we thought we had misunderstood Dr. Love about tapering since neither oncologist seemed concerned. We had to have trust in them.

During this visit, the nurse also mentioned that the x-ray taken the previous week had shown some congestion, such as bronchitis. Erin and I were both very startled as we had been told the x-ray was normal.

In the next two weeks Erin's cough progressed to the point where she was having such severe attacks she could not get her breath. I realize now that she was having broncho-spasms (very serious). Erin was sent in for another x-ray and was put back on Decadron and the breathing problem lessened. We were later told she had radiation pneumonitis which is congestion and inflammation in the radiation field.

Soon after this Erin began having night sweats again and was sent in for another CT scan to determine if the disease had returned, as night sweats are a symptom of Hodgkin's

Disease. The scan showed no return of the disease. Dr. Nichols discussed that perhaps the sweating was due to chemically induced menopause since Erin's periods had ceased.

On May 16, Erin had a follow up visit with Dr. Love, the radiation oncologist at UCSF. I talked with Dr. Love at great length about the steroids Erin had been given, and that they had been abruptly withdrawn, not tapered off, in two separate instances. She expressed great shock that this had been done and said I had been correct, that no one who has had extensive chest radiation should ever be abruptly withdrawn from steroids, regardless of time on them, because it makes radiation pneumonitis flare up and worsen. She said the two doctors should have known better. She also told us, that even though Dr. Gold would be angry with her, she wanted me to make certain Erin was never put on cortisone again once they were able to get her slowly weaned off the drug.

At this time Erin was being tapered off Decadron. Written across the front of her file in *big* black letters, were the words, **NO DECADRON.**

Chapter Six

Erinn Nabong: There is a song by James Taylor that speaks of going through lonely times and of broken dreams but the one thought that never occurs is that you would never see your friend again. Every time I hear that song my eyes well up with tears. I bitterly remember the first time I heard it after Erin's death and it's like it happened yesterday. It takes awhile for the nicer memories to wash away the troubled times. Mostly I remember her voice, her laugh, and her crazy expressions. Erin was always up to any wild antic we would muster up. She was ready and willing to jump in and get it done--whether it was a show, a chore, or a practical joke, which we had plenty of....She was the kind of friend who would always be there when it counted, the kind who was so in tune she would know.

Dates noted are when Erin was writing in her journal

and in some instances are not the actual dates these events occurred:

5-16-89. Telephones are rude. They are loud, obnoxious...rude. They interrupt my thoughts, my conversations, my actions. They are an unpredictable object by theory: no one ever knows when they will ring. It could happen anytime. Anytime! What power it has. But we have power against it. Don't we? Turn off that ringer. Take the receiver off the hook. Turn "the machine" on. DON'T OWN A PHONE. Or let it scream at you. But then it still wins. It is still rude, loud, obnoxious and interruptive.

By theory I say telephones are unpredictable, however in day to day living it does appear that I know when it will scream at me. When I get home, when I'm eating, when I'm relaxing, when I'm having a pleasant conversation or telling a story to my parents....I know, I know, these are the things that fill my days. Obviously what I'm saying is that the phone could ring at just about any given time and I would react the same way. A very unhealthy way, I might add. Why does it affect my mental state to such a strong degree that I am inspired to write all of this at 3:30 a.m.? As I write I keep checking my phone. I like the phone in my room because the ringer is *never* on. Even though it is connected and I can hear the other phones from my room I still have a tolerance for this silent creature.

I'm just one of those people that don't like to talk on the phone. I'll admit that, even though the part I hate most is when it rings and interrupts my life. I'm

O.K. once I'm on—usually. Sometimes I have gotten so upset when someone does call me that I'm too tense to even hold a conversation. That is rare though.

I need to conquer this problem of mine because it is adding absolute, unjustified unneeded stress in my life. It is a ridiculous and destructive behavior— my reaction to a telephone is potentially damaging. It's quite funny that I get so worked up over a telephone. At least I did take a *big* step by telling Lori the truth. Although I could not find it in my heart to say, "Please don't call me as much, you call too often," I did tell her flat out "I HATE to talk on the phone, I cringe every time it rings. I don't even want one when I move out." Of course I will have one. Is that awful? Am I just conforming to society if I have a phone but hate it to such an extreme? Well, yes, in a way I am a conformist but it only shows that I can keep things in perspective. It's okay when I call out. Oh, yes, the phone becomes my friend only when I feel like it. Very selfish indeed. The whole problem is *very* selfish. I should be thrilled that there are people in the world that care enough about me to call me. They are wonderful people not malicious jerks that are trying to wait for the best time of day to make a full felt interruption on my life. I realize all of that but still cannot help my feelings. At least I am not denying my feelings. That would probably do more harm.

With being sick I do have the right to say, "no." Everybody has that right, sick or not, when you get right down to it. My mom insists that I should not feel guilty about not taking calls. She's given it to me in black and white print even. It's not only in the cancer reading but it's popped up in non-illness articles too. I just read *The Art of Selfishness* and have just begun *When I Say No, I Feel Guilty.* Those readings will not help me get over my hatred for the phone but they will reinforce what good ol' Mom keeps telling me: "You're entitled. You're sick. You can say no and not feel guilty." Of course if my stress attacks when the phone rings stem from the fact that (1) it makes me tense to have my parents say I won't take the call because I'm making them do the dirty work and (2) because I can't handle the guilt of not taking the call, then the latter book may help. But mostly for the 2nd reason although with both reasons of stress the underlying factor is guilt. Very interesting discovery I've just made. It's 4:20 a.m. and I think it's time to raid the kitchen. I STILL ENVY THE AMISH.

———————————

Erin had mentioned the Amish several times in those last months, I'm sure she envied the peaceful lifestyle she imagined they were able to enjoy:

———————————

5-15-89. Monday. Went up to school today to tell everyone my decision not to be ASP Chair (smart choice, I might add!). I looked really bad today. I'm not complaining, just telling the facts. My face was extra puffy and fat and my skin looked unhealthy (break out time!). My eyes were listless and puffy (but my mood was O.K.—I wasn't bitching and being depressing or wanting pity or anything). Anyway, Wendy Cole said the nicest thing I've heard in awhile. We hadn't seen each other for a few weeks and she walked into the office, surprised and happy to see me. Then she looked at me and said, "You look tired." I said with a smile, "Yeah, I am." I can't explain how happy it made me that she said that. I don't know if I was more happy that she noticed or happy that she didn't lie and say "You look good" when quite the opposite was true and often is when people say that to me these days. I *really* felt good that she acknowledged that I wasn't looking well. To me, saying that showed her concern and her trying to understand what I'm going thru'. I don't want people to "pity me, pity me" but no one has any idea. Maybe they really don't want to know. They can't do anything about it. Maybe I do want them to "pity me, pity me." But what's wrong with that?

Roni: I thought when someone that I knew well died it would have passed with more. . .well, not excitement, but fanfare. Horns would sound and lights would flash. But that's not how it happened. It was quiet and sad and left an empty place inside anyone who knew her.

5-19-89. It scares me to look in the mirror. That's not me. My face isn't there, it's distorted, it's hidden. Only my eyes speak. Barely. They are crying. There is great pain in my eyes tonight. *My* eyes. The only part of my face that I'll claim right now. That face is not mine. I want to come back! I don't want to scare myself. "Moon Face." That's Mom's scary term for it. She has no idea how those words freak me out. She told me tonight as I was staring at a stranger's reflection, "I didn't think you'd get the moon face so fast. I didn't think that happened unless you were on it (steroids) for months and months." Yeah, well, lucky me. Poor Mom, I love her so much. Dad, too. I didn't want him to see me like I was today. Today was bad. Never took a shower. Cried spontaneously for absolutely no reason throughout the day. My face/physical appearance has never been worse. I regretted that Mom had to be around but she's more used to it. I just kept thinking about poor Dad having to see his daughter so sick looking. I'm remembering our first trip to UCSF when we passed a cancer patient on a gurney. We couldn't tell his/her sex. She/he was bald, moon faced—and Dad said, "That person is really sick." It wasn't the words but the emotion that I got from him that will always stick in my mind. I don't ever want him to have to have that horrible feeling when he looks at me. He would have had that horrible feeling today had I not had to go to the emergency room. (Oh, I know he's had pretty horrible feelings when he's looked at me—after surgery, in and out of the hospital—and I don't mean horrible as in bad. No, not bad. More like very sad I have to be sick. That's what I mean. But you know I'm not writing this for anyone but me so I have no idea why I'm trying to explain it. I know exactly what I mean.) Anyway, having to go into E.R. saved my dad. Although I still looked bad I at least had rinsed my body in the shower and put on eyeliner and mascara. I looked like ape-shit at best when I went to the hospital but Mom said I looked 100% better than I had during the day. Whoa, that's pretty bad!

You know I told her tonight that we should take pictures of me because right now is the worst that I will ever look in my life (it had better be at least!) and in one year I will be looking my best. I know this is true. I will be healthy, radiant, self-confident, healthy, in shape, beautiful and HEALTHY. I know this is only a small period of my life and I've learned before from living in Alameda that you have to be at your worst before you can be at your best. I've hit rock bottom now but, by God, I'm going to be a stud after this!!

Shortly after Erin's graduation from high school we moved to Alameda from the Sacramento area. She had to leave her close network of friends, and her sister who had opted to stay and finish college, and it was a very difficult transition for her. She attended a commuter college in a nearby town and none of the friends she made lived near us. The three of us started doing many more things together, such as walking the Golden Gate Bridge, visiting tide pools at Half Moon Bay, attending movies, going to dinner, etc., and she really got to know her father and me as people instead of parents and she liked what she saw. We became very close friends.

May 19, we made a visit to the emergency room. Erin had a small pimple on her laparotomy scar and had been using hot packs per Dr. Love's advice. That afternoon the pimple had drained about two tablespoons of pus, so Erin called Dr. Gold. He exclaimed, "Whoa, that's not my responsibility," and told her that she would have to see Dr. White, the surgeon who had performed Erin's surgery four months prior to this time.

We met with Dr. White at the hospital where blood work was done. The doctor decided the pimple was an abscessed stitch and said to continue using the hot packs and see him if there was any change. Erin was not given medication and had no further problems. On May 21, her dose of Decadron was dropped to 6 mg. per day but her breathing problem was back and she had to rest several times when navigating the stairs to her bedroom. Also, Erin's night sweats were increasing. During this time period she had told Dr. Gold that her breathing problem was so severe that she was having difficulty walking from one room to another. His comment was, "Just stay in one room, Erin." She turned to me as we left his office and said, "Does he ever know when to be serious?":

5-21-89. Sunday. I hate Sundays. Always have, always will. I'm in a shitty mood. I'm really unhappy. I was fine this morning when my parents and I went to watch "Bay to Breakers" [a foot race in San Francisco] at 6:30 a.m. I slept all afternoon yesterday then took a sleeping pill last night and luckily it worked. I just happened to wake up at 5:28 a.m. with a night sweat and it was time to get up and I felt rested. (I've been having a lot of night sweats lately. Two last night. I keep a towel hanging on my bed post. I dry myself off with it and then lay on it and for some reason laying on the towel is better than being on the sheets because I guess it absorbs the sweat instead of just letting it be wet. One night a few weeks ago I was up about seven times with the sweats. I even had to get another chest CT scan done because we all thought my cancer had come back. It hasn't, though. I think it's the fucking steroids doing it. I HATE THOSE THINGS.) Back to today—I was fine at the race but in the car ride home I could feel a change occurring. Not a good change either. By the time I got home and into my room my mind "clicked." That's what it's been doing lately. It just goes "click" you are out of control. I sat and cried and cried for no reason. Then I do this weird thing of having to have everything in my room organized and put away. I get all spacey and I can't think of or do anything else until it is in order. Maybe—yes, I think this is it—I do that because I feel the need to have order and be in control because I know at those times I have no control over what is happening in my mind. It's the steroids. I'm not a weak person. This is beyond my control and it scares me to death.

I stayed upstairs away from Mom and Dad because I knew I would be mean because of the crazed state I was in. Not crazed as in running around throwing things, but crazed in the sense of a true manic depressive or schizo. I moved pretty slowly but always with purpose. When my purpose stopped, so would I. That seems to get me very upset, not having anything to do. Sure, I could read, play guitar, watch T.V., call someone, take a walk, sit outside, write (like I'm finally doing now), etc., etc. But none of those things make me feel like I have a purpose. Things like cleaning up, doing laundry, organizing—those things are what my mind wants me to be doing when I get in those weird moods. It's my mind's way of saying, "I may be totally fucking with you, you can't help it, you hate it, you have no control. BUT do this and this and subconsciously you will be in control." I don't know, It's all pretty weird but it does seem to make sense. Funny thing is I hadn't made any of these connections until I started writing. I'm scared. I really am scared. I don't want to feel like this all summer. I don't want to be depressed next fall. I'm so scared. So scared.

I got a bank statement today. I haven't written a check in months—probably not since last year! The monthly service charge is $5. I wouldn't let my mom close the checking account because I felt like I would be losing a major part of my independence. That checking account means the world to me. Today I realized that it's crazy to keep it open because I'm not going to have an income (a job) till probably next December or something. I'm not going to be writing any checks. I've got to face the facts. I'm going to be at home next year so I'll never buy groceries. Oh, but God, what about things at school like paying for registration and parking, etc., etc. Well those are the only things I can think of and I guess it's not worth the service charge just to keep my insecurities comforted. Maybe we could close it for the summer and then make a decision. I'm keeping my savings though because I will sell that car someday soon and put that $$ in there. Sell that car. That's another part of my independence that will be gone. I haven't driven it since the "Night Ranger" incident in Cupertino (except back from the shop in Novato).

Erin, her sister Lizz, and a good friend, Robert Jones, had driven Erin's little green Honda Civic (called "The Fish

Bowl" by her friends) to a Night Ranger concert and the transmission had gone out on the way. They had called us and said they were getting a hotel room and for me to come get them the next morning, which I did.

Early the following day, Robert rented a trailer to haul the car back to Novato and he and Erin started for Cupertino. Mid-afternoon they arrived back, minus her car. They were driving down busy 19th Avenue in San Francisco when Robert glanced in the rearview mirror and saw the trailer proceeding to pass the truck he and Erin were in. The hitch had broken, also the safety chain, and the trailer went speeding down the street, sheered off a fire hydrant and came to a stop, with water shooting into the air from the broken hydrant. At this point Erin vowed never to drive her car again:

That was December 2. Now it's May 21. It was my choice not to drive it. It's unsafe, bad luck, all that— but at least right now I can say that I have a car. I have a car but I'm trying to sell it. When it's sold, I'll use my parent's car. Just like I use my parent's house, money, emotions, anything and everything. Yes, I feel rotten about that! But I didn't bring this God damn sickness on. Fuck, I'm so angry right now. My emotions change with each gust of wind.

On May 23, Erin's breathing attacks were back in full force. Decadron was raised to 8 mg. and she was sent in for another x-ray which showed more congestion—diagnosis still radiation pneumonitis. No other tests were considered, such as a sputum sample or a pulmonary function test, even though the study Erin was in had specifically mentioned pulmonary function tests would be given, if indicated, because of the risks associated with bleomycin.

On May 26, Erin had increasing breathing difficulty and I called Dr. Love at UCSF, who indicated that I should insist the oncologist see Erin as this could get serious very fast. (I later discovered in my research that radiation pneumonitis can be fatal.) Dr. Love said the Decadron would have to be tapered off even *more* slowly and it would probably take six months to get Erin completely off this drug. We immediately went in to see Dr. Gold, who teased Erin about her fat face (a side effect of the steroids), saying she had cute little chipmunk cheeks. I can still see the pain in her eyes caused by that remark. Was he not aware of how sensitive a young woman of twenty feels when she sees the devastating effects of a drug every time she looks in a mirror? Dr. Gold decided to increase the Decadron to 16 mg. for three days and then drop it back down to 12 mg. At this suggestion Erin said, "16 mg.?", and asked if it was harmful to go from 16 mg. to 12 mg. so quickly. He said no, which startled us because Dr. Love had specifically stated the dosage would have to be tapered very slowly or the pneumonitis would worsen. After some thought, Dr. Gold decided to increase the dosage to 12 mg. Erin was not sent in for an x-ray at this time.

As we were leaving the office Dr. Gold told Erin, "Don't

worry, Erin, this breathing problem is just bothersome, it won't get serious." (Ironically, these were the last words he ever spoke to our daughter. He was away on vacation at the time of her death.) The increase in Decadron alleviated the breathing problem somewhat but Erin was still having some difficulty.

When Erin went in for chemo on May 30, the doctor's office was in a complete uproar. To us, it seemed as if everyone was angry and impatient. They were in the process of getting ready to move to a new office and were trying to get organized. Dr. Gold was on vacation so Dr. Nichols was handling the entire case load.

Bleomycin was eliminated from this particular dose of chemo because of Erin's lung problems. She was sent in for another x-ray at this time. No other tests were suggested, although there was some discussion of sending her to a lung specialist but this was not done.

Around this time Erin had a menstrual period, so chemical menopause was eliminated as a reason for her ever increasing night sweats. It was decided that she was probably having a reaction to the Decadron. (I now know that night sweats are a symptom of pneumocystis carinii pneumonia, as well as an indication of other lung problems.) At this visit Erin also showed the nurse some white-heads that were appearing on her leg:

I WANT TO BE IN CONTROL. For the first time thru' all of this I want to scream, "This isn't fair." I can tolerate all this other shit that has happened to me-the cancer itself, the moon face, the horrible aches and pains from chemo, the hair loss from radiation, the itching, the joint pain and swelling and on and on and on. I can handle it and I haven't thought "Why me? Why me?" I've dealt with it all. But I can't handle what these steroids are doing to my mental state. IT'S NOT FAIR! It's beyond my control. But, you know, everything else has been too. But when your head gets fucked up nothing matters because you can't think clearly enough to realize that—fuck, I don't know. You know the shitty thing is that I'm on these steroids because of shortness of breath and breathing attacks. And yes, the horrible side effects of steroids—mental anguish and all—are better than having those breathing attacks. They were fucking scary. So I've been on these steroids for awhile and am slowly tapering off them each week (was taking 3 a day, now 1 1/2) and guess what I've discovered this weekend? I can't climb the fucking stairs without having to rest! This is just fantastic. So basically I'm going thru' absolute hell by taking these steroids that are supposed to let me breathe normally and have suddenly stopped doing their job. Is that a kick in the pants or what? Fuck, I mean how chipper can a person be? You know I hadn't originally planned to write like this—to myself in such a "journal" fashion. I like it though. It helps me to write this all out.

Oh, I should write about my psycho experience this afternoon. I came downstairs finally and Mom was in the kitchen. My mood was bad and I wasn't about to talk to her. She said pleasantly, "You're sure jerking around." I snapped and growled out a muttered, "No, I'm not." I made my infamous fake cheese quesadillas and sat at the kitchen table eating quickly and angrily. Finished and just sat with a horribly mean look on my face. None of this was on purpose. I swear to God I had no control over any of it. My body was tense and shaking as I sat in silence with the look on my face getting more psycho and emotional as my mind raced with bizarre thoughts. I was almost in a complete emotional upheaval because I couldn't think of anything to eat. There was *no* food in this house. Emotions were building. Mom was still in the kitchen. She didn't say a word and I didn't look at her once but I know she kept looking at me not sure what would happen next. I got up, got some ice water and the Chips Ahoy. I sat down and started cramming the cookies into my mouth, crying, and thinking the whole time, "This is the only thing to fucking eat. These cookies are the only thing in this house to eat." Totally psycho. It was very scary. I wasn't weeping but tears were running like a river and snot was building up. I put my left hand to my head to try to let my mom know that I wasn't doing it for her benefit—that I didn't want her to see it (but the food was in the kitchen and that's where she was). I didn't look at her but she had moved and pretended to be reading something at the kitchen stairs. She was watching me carefully and with deep concern. I had taken 2 half-full packages of cookies (equal 1 package) and finished them. Immediately after finishing the last cookie I changed again. The tears stopped. I felt calmer, and "the look" on my face was gone. For the first time I looked at my mom. She glanced up with terror and concern in her eyes, not knowing if she should be looking at me or not (when I caught her eye she was ready to look away if I had still had "the look"). I calmly said, "Can you hear if the dryer is still going?" Total scitzo (however you spell it).

Chapter Seven

Jon: I find myself wondering if other people saw the same things in Erin that I did. I guess I don't really care. My feelings towards Erin are very personal. I still have very strong feelings about her and I believe her tragedy is not only the loss of what she was but what she certainly would have been. Not could have--would have. I can't believe the tears still come so easily...I haven't mentioned her capacity for love, her courage, or the inspiration she gave me, but I trust you will.

5-23-89. My shortness of breath/breathing attacks are back in full force all right. Each day it gets worse and it is now almost to the point it was before. I couldn't even speak to the doctors about it today because I couldn't get my breath long enough to talk on the phone. Mom talked to Mary [oncology nurse] and Michelle Vincent. Mary talked to Dr. Gold but we couldn't reach Dr. Love (my only hope to get off steroids). My worst nightmare has come true: they've all decided to raise my steroid dose back up to 8 mg. a day at least until next Tuesday (chemo) when they will make a final decision or something. I was on 6 mg. and in two days I was going to be able to cut it to 4 mg. Now, up to 8 with no tapering in sight for a while—at least that's how I see it. Even if they do give me an alternative to steroids for this breathing problem—which I'm counting on Dr. Love to come up with—I will still have to come back down gradually from my new dose of 8 mg. a day. It's just that much longer on this horrible drug. Today my chest x-ray did show more congestion than the first two. I guess it's radiation pneumonitis. My physical appearance has absolutely gone to hell. The zits are getting worse, I've gained about 15 pounds, my upper body is looking "buff" (and not in a good way), and the facial hair is rapidly increasing. I had to "trim" my face about a half hour ago. I'm having a hard time accepting this steroid increase. There's got to be something else. God, and the breathing. I can't go anywhere and I can't exercise off my fat. Roni is coming to visit tomorrow. I warned her of my appearance and my breathing but I know she will be shocked. I will feel so bad if I have the breathing problems like I had when I went to see Kim. [This was in April when she had her first really severe breathing attack.] Kim wanted to come over for yesterday and today but I told her no. I kinda felt guilty but it was the right thing to do. I don't want her to see me like that again. Plus now would be even worse because my physical appearance is so "distressing." The worst is going to be facing *Jim. I haven't seen him for so long. I'm so embarrassed about the way I look. He's going to be really upset but he won't show it. He doesn't really know how to deal with this. I talked with him tonight and was really short of breath. I was complaining about the steroids and stuff and he was agreeing that it really sucked. He had wanted to take me out to dinner at some point before he goes to Florida. No way. I liked the idea when he first brought it up but now I'm thinking I don't want to be anybody's date to anything. I'm gross right now and don't want to have to pretend like I'm not. I don't want him to have to be seen with me and I don't want to be seen in public trying to pass as "looking good on a date." Also, now with the breathing, I can see myself not even being able to order or choking on food or something. Bad scene. So instead he's just gonna come over—probably Saturday—and just hang out . My parents are getting out of the house so that will be easier. It's hard enough to see Jim just because of our past, but I'm worried that this is just going to be mind-blowingly difficult.

I was just writing that outside on the back stairs but it was too cold (8:15 p.m. on a May night—should be warmer!) so I came up to my room. Having to sit and catch my breath. I'm wondering if it's a mistake to have Roni visit. Well, I did warn her.

I'm reading *Your Erroneous Zones* now. [Erin loved this book.] I read something last night that I already knew was true but it upset me nonetheless. Perhaps seeing it in black and white was the problem. It was saying how the two things a person can say that will always get the worst reaction (or create negative feelings or something like that) is when-1-

they say they are tired and-2-they say they are not feeling well.

Need I say more about what is so disturbing about this? Well I will try to explain it to myself since I'm the only one reading this and maybe I can figure something out in the process. For the past 6 months or so I have been sick. This is a fact. I don't consider it to be one of those "I'm" labels that the book talks about. They use that as an example too: You "label" yourself, "I'm sick" or "I'm tired" therefore you think you can't change or something.

When people ask me how I am, do they really want to know? I've decided that, no, they don't. At school, acquaintances like C.A. and Bryan ask how I'm doing and I refuse to lie and say "Great, never been better!" So I give 'em a fake smile and say "I'm doing O.K." Even that is a lie most of the time because I really want to scream and say "I feel SHIT-TY most of the time including right now. You have no idea how hard all of this is. I wish you all could understand that I'm not over-reacting to what's happening in my life right now. This is heavy shit. Why don't you understand that!" But of course I don't say that. But God, nothing else is really going on in my life right now so how can I not talk to people about the way I feel (back to the book now). It's really hard. I think that may be *one* of the reasons why I rather keep to myself. It's hard to be around people. I don't have much to talk about regarding myself except my health. I know people are uncomfortable hearing about it. They can't do anything to help me. They don't know what to say because they don't truly understand. God, I've written about this before but I guess it's because it really bugs me. During phone

calls to Robert, Kim, Roni, and now Jim, I start talking about what's happening with me either because
they ask, or in the case of Jim, and Roni and Kim for
that matter, I need to explain like why I can't do this
or that or why I don't want visitors but it just comes
out sounding like complaining and self-pity. It's a
bad scene that I'm going thru' and I try to make light
of it as best I can with these people but this shit sucks
and I'm telling them. But I try to laugh about it at the
same time. Still I know it's hard for the person at the
other end. But it's hard for me, too.

I'm just about ready to cry right now because I'm
so hungry. I'm feeling out of control more and more
each day and that must be stopped. That's scary.
Here's what I've eaten today: around 7 a.m.—2 waf-
fles, hot chocolate, two slices of bread, fruit cocktail.
Around 10:30 a.m.—3 pieces of French toast, bowl of
melons. Around 12:30 p.m.—big bowl of ricearoni
and three choc. chip cookies. Around 1:30 or 2
p.m.—huge deli sandwich from Safeway. (Then I
stopped eating because I took a nap), dinner around
7 which was the original Mom stir-fry w/white rice.
Apparently wasn't enough because it is now 8:45
p.m. and I am absolutely famished. No joke. And
each time that I ate today I was in extreme *need* of
food. You know, *really* HUNGRY. Fucking steroids.

I think what's happening now is that I'm really
freaking out about my eating, weight gain, all
around horrible appearance because before I kept
telling myself, "This is only temporary. Soon you
will be off the steroids and things will gradually get
back to normal. Your face will go back to normal,
your appetite will be under control so you can begin
to lose weight, etc., etc." But now I see it temporari-

ly turning into something much too permanent for my liking. When I say permanent I don't mean forever but anything like 2 or 3 months. If I'm on steroids for that long I won't be able to leave the house because I'll look so bad. Of course, if my breathing problems clear up I can get out and start walking again. That is if my granny knees don't lock up like they have been doing. At this point I'm thinking that if I can breathe normally but have to be on steroids and my knees are in poor shape, that I must sacrifice my knees, endure the pain and make myself get out and walk on them even if I move at a snail's pace. I'm so hungry. I'm so fat. I'm so scared.

Lori: We used to make these huge sundaes (ice cream, syrup, whip cream, and M & Ms) during any time we were stressed. People couldn't believe we would eat them, they were so big, but we did, with a big smile on our faces all the way through it. Erin didn't cook very often but food sure made her happy. It was so weird to see her so happy about food. Especially because she was not fat.

5-26-89. Friday. Yesterday I was supposed to be down to 4 mg. of steroids a day. Boy, that would have been great, eh? But as I wrote earlier (I think it was Tuesday) I was increased to 8 mg. That really bummed me out. Well today, Friday, my breathing was much worse. Hmmm. That shouldn't happen since I increased the steroids. Mom talked to Dr. Love and she said there are no alternatives now and that I will probably have to increase the dose again and taper off so slowly that I will be on steroids for *six months*. Oh my. She also said that this breathing problem can get worse real fast and that I should insist that Dr. Gold see me today before the 3 day Memorial Day weekend. She said it could get to the point of hospitalization fast if nothing was done (or something along that line).

So my mom called Mary and hauled my ass down to the doctor's office. Dr. Gold made fun of my fat face, listened to my chest and increased my steroids to 16 mg. a day for about 3 days and then down to 12 mg. daily. I said, "16 mg.!" Then I asked if that was bad to go from 16 to 12 so quickly. He said, "No." Whoa. I gave my mom a look. I don't have a spleen, dude! Have you been listening to Dr. Love? She just said I'd have to be tapered off even slower than before to make sure this radiation pneumonitis doesn't come back. Then Dr. Gold decided not to do that, and he just said take 12 mg. Oh, well, that's better. God, yesterday I was supposed to be down to 4 mg. now I'm up to 12 with the knowledge that for 6 months I will be taking the "drug from hell." Wow, right now I'm so fucked up and wired from the stuff that I'm just dealing with it. I'm using some of that shit from *Your Erroneous Zones* about this situation being "unfortunate" not "unfair." It's all in the way you look at things. Ha! Ha!

Funny thing—I don't often look at the paper but I happened to pick it up tonight right before I wrote this and lo and behold I flip right to an Ann Landers column with the lead line "Ann tells a tragic tale of steroid use." Oh great, Ann, do tell. It was about a high school athlete who shot up with them. He got all suicidal and shit because steroids fuck your brain up so much. He also lost his hair. Whoa, I don't want to hear that especially after yesterday when I was pulling clumps out. Weird, it was just yesterday (or maybe the day before). It wasn't coming out like w/radiation but it was like breaking or something. I shouldn't have been yanking at it but I was like looking for something to freak out about or something. My hair is really gross these days and it is thinning quite a bit. The flatness of it frames my moon face in such a flattering way, too!

I remember later explaining to Erin the difference in anabolic steroids and the type she was taking:

Anyway, I was bummed w/David today because he just didn't seem to know what was going on. He even told me, "This isn't anything to get real worried about. It's not serious, it just makes you feel lousy." (Not an exact quote, of course, but very close.) Bullshit it's not serious. Was he just trying to make me feel better or does he really believe that? Mary was really bummed that I had to increase the steroids 'cuz she knows how they mess me up. So does Dr. Love.

I met *Angela today. [A young woman also suffering from Hodgkin's Disease who had called to talk to Erin. Erin wasn't in the mood to talk and never returned her call.] The lady that called my mom and I never called her. She was getting chemo. She looked great. I looked like hell—FAT moon face—and she told me I looked good (I hate that) but she didn't know what I looked like before. After she said that my mom mentioned the steroids.

I'm not making much sense tonight. I'm having

trouble with this but I wanted to comment on something else. I'm getting whiteheads on my legs and it's pretty gross.

Oh, also last night I woke up and immediately thought "Johnny Carson died." I even asked my mom this morning if she read it in the paper. I'm watching Carson right now and he was talking about Memorial Day weekend and other recent things so I guess he's alive (well that was stupid. I'm sure this isn't live—well it might be) but anyway, I hope he doesn't die 'cuz that would be weird. I miss *Jonathan. [A friend from high school days whom she had lost track of after he was discharged from the service.]

Kim Church: I refuse to believe that our friendship has ceased to exist simply because Erin has ceased to exist in any tangible way for me to know for sure if she is here. But what is for sure? How can I prove a "sense," an "aura" of familiarity? Western Rationality has for too long imprisoned my beliefs that life only exists from the cradle to the grave. But I know her uncaptured spirit stirs restless in the universe.

5-27-89. It's about midnight and I just got thru' reading all of Jonathan's letters. I also arranged them chronologically. Those letters mean so much to me. The first ones were written back in the summer of '86 and the last ones—the most touching, the most meaningful—were written in the spring of '88. It is now close to the summer of '89 and I miss him terribly. I think of him often.

During my radiation treatments my mom and I started driving home by way of the end of Haight Street. Everyday we would pass that little lake in

Golden Gate Park across from the McDonald's at the end of Haight. That day that Jonathan and I met there was the last time that I saw him. I rode BART in from Alameda and then rode a bus to that spot. The bus is significant and I don't need to write why. But wait. Where did Jonathan and I go in my car when I picked him up at BART in Mom's car, got gas, and was upset with him because he didn't want to go see my house and my mom? Why can't I remember where we went? It must've been the city but I don't even remember driving in the—wait. We went to the zoo and *that* was the last time I saw him. It was awkward for some reason. I remember I drove him home to Pleasanton afterward. That was it. I have no idea how he feels about me now. Right before my major surgery in January when I was getting my last drinking in with Erinn Nabong and Wendy Cole, I called his mother. It was 3:30 a.m. and I was very drunk. I didn't sound drunk though. I think I was very serious and I even told her my full name. She said he had moved to Sacramento and she didn't have his phone number. It was a mistake to call that late because now if I call back to try to get some info she surely won't be responsive. That was many months ago though. She probably thinks (or thought) I'm pregnant with his child! I told Lizz to try to help me find him—to ask Z., D.M., anyone that might know where he is. I miss him so much. He means so much to me. He will always have a deep place within me. Hopefully that will not have to be only memories and letters. I want him back in my life. I'm so curious about what and how he's doing. I'm *so* hoping that he has continued in a positive growth process. He changed so much thru' those few years. He learned so much about himself. I hope to God he didn't regress. I love him dearly.

I read the Jim Morrison book *No One Here Gets Out Alive* and thought of him constantly throughout my reading. Today I looked up Arthur Rumbaud's name in the encyclopedia to find out more about this person that Jonathan often mentioned. I got the name of a book of his memoirs and am determined to find it, buy it, and read it and read it until I understand it. I have a feeling it will be pretty intellectual, deep, and a bit hard for me to follow but I want to understand. Jonathan has spoken of Lenny Bruce often and I don't know much about him. I'm going to try to find a book about him, too.

I want to get in contact with Jonathan again not because I have (had) cancer and want him to know. In fact I would be very frightened to tell him for fear of his reaction. I have no idea what he would think. Would he think I just wanted to let him know so he could feel sorry for me or guilty that we haven't stayed in touch? I don't want that. I just want to talk with him. I really want to see him but I don't want him to see me this way.

I'm wondering if my coming face to face with a life threatening illness has made me realize how truly important it is not to lose a relationship like Jonathan and I had. Things can happen so quickly. Life can change or end so abruptly. I've learned that for sure. But I think I would want to reach Jonathan again even if this hadn't happened. I just have so much time to think about it (him). Maybe that's it but I can't deny what I feel when I read his letters. They make me melt just as they did when I first received them. After one especially sentimental letter I received in Alameda I remember telling my mother that I thought I was falling in love with him. He is such a special person. Not many people see that. Not even his own mother. But what is he like now? What if he's living with a woman? What if he's back on drugs? I'm sure he still smokes. Major bummer. Does he still go to AA meetings? What kind of friends does he hang out with? What's his music scene these days? Is he working in a medical profession? Is he happy? Does he think about me? Does he miss me? Do I still hold a special place in his heart like he told me in his last letters? I want to know these things.

My mom said something like, "It would be a shame if you lost contact with him forever." I abruptly said something like, "That won't happen, it can't happen. We'll get in touch with each other." I have to, too, and I will. I want him to know how I still feel about him—that is if he hasn't completely turned into something different. But for some reason I have a feeling that when we meet up again it may be very special. I'm hoping for that.

I can't help wondering if he will pull back because of my health problems or want to "nurture" me and be closer. Obviously the latter would be pleasant.

Kim: I have continued to find answers about Death through visions of Erin's life. Words cannot do justice to her presence in the kitchen making her mom laugh, or at a Night Ranger concert drinking and being obnoxious, or in our friendship creating the future by talking about the future. No, only moments filled with bursts of energy could give a sense of Erin's presence, which was felt by all. She was a funny young woman who was incredibly expressive and opinionated, with a passion for communicating her emotions. Whether those emotions were joy or frustration, excitement or boredom, euphoria or depression, she was always open and honest when she felt it was important to be so. Of course, there was a serious side to Erin that allowed her to become more philosophical about issues. And because she was so caring and concerned, she could become stubborn and difficult.

She had no problems making waves, felt sure about standing her ground, and could always count on her persistence to get through to people. On the other side of Erin lived a silly goof who danced wherever she was, simply because she felt the music "moved" her. She loved to make people laugh and had a spirit that demanded attention. She was overt in her facial expressions, and in fact rarely hid her reactions to life. I often wondered where she got all of her energy.

5-28-89. Big revelation here. I picked up my bass for the first time in quite a while and as I was messing around with it my thoughts wandered to Jack since he actually inspired me to buy the bass. I thought about how he went to New York to audition for a new band. New York. Six months ago that would have sent me into hysterics because I would have thought he was going to move there. That idea crossed my mind today and I thought, "Oh well, I'll live." My God, Night Ranger has broken up. I never cried, lit candles, played their videos or records in tribute—nothing! I accepted it.

In today's pink [entertainment] section it showed that Brad Gillis is in a new band, M-1, which will be giving their debut performance this Saturday at the OMNI. I'd like to go check it out but I'm not going to. I will always love Night Ranger. They will always be my favorite band. I'm not obsessed with Jack anymore. There I said it. I'm over him. I know we aren't going to get married. I was wrong all those years. I knew there was some reason for my obsession with that man and the band. There was some reason why everything that happened to me was connected with them. There was a reason I kept hanging on. I thought it was my destiny to be with Jack. I was wrong. Night Ranger saved my life. It was almost as if the band was created just for that purpose. They strung me along for years. My passion and obsession grew to outrageous proportions. Night Ranger, specifically Jack, were/was one of the most important aspects of my life for quite a few years. *Few* things made me happier. *Few* things compared in importance. The stress that went with the SSU N.R. show couldn't have been brought on by much of anything else, as I see it. Only a death or serious illness in my family would have caused me that kind of stress. The stress is what made my cancerous lump swell up so I could detect it. Night Ranger saved my life. For all I know, if that concert thing hadn't happened—all that stress due to my passion for that band—I could still be walking around with the cancer spreading silently throughout my body. Night Ranger broke up shortly after I found out about my disease. It was like, "O.K., we saved Erin's life. We did our job, now it's time to go on." My mom believes they saved my life also. She hopes I get a chance to talk with Jack about it sometime. I do too but it would be a heavy conversation because I'd be trying to convince him that I wasn't a psychopath! Ha. Ha.

This day stands out very clearly in my mind. Erin covered Jack Blades' picture with a picture of her sister; neither of us said a word. I remember feeling proud of her but I also recall having a feeling of dread:

So something very, very good has come from my having cancer. I have rid myself of an overbearing obsession that in many ways was holding me back in some aspects of my life. I am free but I will always admire and love Jack and Night Ranger. I have no heroes now. No one to worship and it feels good.

During the night prior to her June 7 chemo Erin's breathing problems had worsened. At her appointment the following morning she told Dr. Nichols that her breathing difficulty had increased. Under protest from Erin (she writes of this in her journal), Dr. Nichols reduced the Decadron from 12 mg. to 10 mg. She said it was important for Erin to get off the cortisone and that 2 mg. a day would not make that much difference. To us it was strange to reduce the dosage when the problem was worsening. Erin had taken a walk (very slowly) the night before, and we both felt that Dr. Nichols thought this was an indication that everything was better. She did not seem to really listen to what Erin was telling her that morning. Dr. Nichols told Erin the dosage could be bumped up if the need arose, and she did not order an x-ray because Erin had had one the previous week and she decided another was unnecessary so soon. (The entire staff appeared tired to us that morning. They had spent the weekend painting and moving into the new office.)

The whitehead on Erin's leg had now developed into a full scale sore which looked very bad. She told Dr. Nichols that she was putting hot packs on it and that it was draining pus. Dr. Nichols appeared angry, said heat was okay but not to drain it, she would do it if it was necessary. No medication was given.

I remember that after one of Erin's last appointments she turned to me as we went to the car and said, "Maxine doesn't like me anymore." I asked her why she would think that and her reply was, "She doesn't hug me anymore now that I'm fat." I'm sure Dr. Nichols did not realize that she had always before greeted Erin with a hug but had not done so that day. Unfortunately, that was a day when a hug was badly needed because Erin was so conscious of her deteriorating physical appearance.

The chemo on June 7 made Erin as sick as the first time, even though the bleomycin had been removed. The breathing problem worsened and Erin took it upon herself to increase the dosage to 12 mg. as the doctor had stated she could do. We knew it always took several days for the steroid to be effective so she just took it easy and gave it a chance to work. This was simple to do since Erin felt so badly from the chemo and because she was out of breath whenever she moved around.

We were very angry with the doctors at this point

because none of this seemed to be taken seriously by them. Erin and I were going to be on their doorstep early Monday morning demanding some answers and action. All weekend I kept asking her if maybe we shouldn't call the doctors but she said no, we would wait until Monday since they wouldn't do anything anyway. At this point Erin had lost all trust in them. I found out later from one of her friends that Erin had tried to protect her father and me and had kept from us how very badly she felt at that time.

Chapter Eight

&rinn: I miss her desperately, if only because I was counting on her to share all the "old times" with as we grew older. Fish would be the old college buddy that my kids would be sick of hearing about. Ever since that day in June, I make sure that everything I do is exactly what I want it to be. There is no holding back, no waiting for things to happen. I gotta get out there and do it, enjoy it, LIVE. I'll be damned if her death was for nothing. She was and is by far too special.

5-29-89. It's Monday night, probably around midnight. I don't really want to know. I watched "Apocalypse Now" and then "Valley Girl" tonight. "Valley Girl" is on my Night Ranger tape so I'm just letting that play now. I haven't watched those Night Ranger videos and interviews in quite a while. I'm still okay though when I see them.

I don't want to go to bed tonight after trying to

sleep in a puddle of sweat all last night. God, that is so gross. The sheets and blanket got soaked as well as my poor body. My head always feels the worst—it's where my bald spot in back is that feels grossest when sweaty. Anyway, I'm not looking forward to that happening again tonight. I'm not even tired right now but I know I need to sleep. Tomorrow is chemo—oh boy! I'd like to be rested just for that, but also I know that I'll probably be taking Percocet by the end of the week [for muscle and joint pain caused by chemo] so I won't be sleeping then. I refuse to take the sleeping pills every night (for one reason when you do that your body becomes immune and they stop working).

Today I talked with poor old *Randy Stevens who has such a horrible life. Ha. Ha. It was the first time I'd talked with him since he was "denied" the position of concerts chair for the 2nd year. I was afraid to talk to him about [it] since I was on the interviewing committee. The others never even told me about K.'s interview. I guess they expected I'd be around that day for the last ASP meeting although I haven't gone to one since before chemo and I only went to one before that! I couldn't breathe anyway so even if they would've called spur of the moment for me to come to the interview I wouldn't have...I told him things would get better and he moaned, "Well at this point they can't get any worse." Then he asks me, "So what have you been up to?" Oh well, Randy, nothing much. I can't breathe you know so I don't leave the house and can barely go from room to room.

I spend my nights drowning in sweat and that's about it. Fuck, how in the hell can anybody complain to me about anything? Let's put things into perspective here! Oh, and Randy, you're seeing a girl at the moment and are very happy with the situation. I, however, am so disgusted with my physical self that even if I could go out and do things I wouldn't want to! I've gained about 20 pounds and I have a fucking moon face! I can't exercise because I can't breathe!! And it wouldn't matter if I wasn't eating anything in regards to my puffy face because it's out of my control. Steroid side effects. So Randy tell me more about how miserable you are and how awful life is. I love to hear it really—it's great. I can really feel for you....Can you tell I have a bit of animosity in me tonight? It's not just tonight, it's quite often because people can be so stupid!

This young man was an extremely close friend of Erin's and because of this closeness it was a common occurrence for them to share the good and bad times. Erin had a knack of helping her friends with their problems, always ready and willing to listen and help in any way possible. But at this point she was dealing with a life or death situation, also with the deterioration of her physical self, and feeling anger at the entire predicament. Erin let very few of those around her know how ill she really was feeling or how frightened she was. There was no way for anyone to understand what she was undergoing unless they had also gone through a similar situation. For Randy, the conversation they were having was as their conversations had always been, but for Erin life was, of course, no longer the same. I am sure most of the animosity she was feeling was anger at the state she found herself in, a circumstance where she was being swept along with no control whatsoever over what was happening to her and no one, including myself, had any inkling of what she was experiencing:

At least today I was able to get out of the house. The folks and I tried to catch a matinee of the 3rd Indiana Jones movie. Everyone else in Marin County also wanted to spend their Memorial Day that way so we ended up going out to breakfast and then to a winery (with wild mountain goats).

Kim: Just weeks before she died, Erin called me depressed and bored. She couldn't drive anymore, and asked me if I would come and take her to the beach. Our last trip together was to Point Reyes, a small beach up Northern California's coast. It was rather chilly, and we bundled up to walk to the lighthouse, which was several hundred yards away from the car. Erin grew tired very fast, and had difficulty with even the slowest of pace. We were both frustrated with her weakness. For me, it was weird to see Erin, who is such a restless ball of energy, drain in front of my eyes. For her, she dreaded the absence of her normal self. We talked about a time when she wouldn't be lethargic; when she would have the energy to laugh; when she would want to spend her days living, not just existing.

6-3-89
Pain and suffering
Always for a reason
To suffer is to grow
Without pain nothing is learned
To grow is to change
Change should be constant
For without change
Life would be stagnant
Pain and suffering
Always for a reason
Look to them
They are positive forces in life

Kelly: Erin not only demanded diversity of experience but encouraged us to push our limits.

6-3-89.
View From the Open Window at Night
A constant flow of moving lights
come and go in different patterns
Origin, destination, purpose
Unknown
Hello white
Goodbye red
The sight soothes
The hum calms

Stacey Wagner: It's her smile and her laughter that I remember most. In her short life, Erin laughed a lot.

6-3-89.
Spider, spider on my wall
Who invited you
I know I didn't call
You're big and crispy
I think spiders are bad
Get out of my room
Before I scream for my DAD
Your legs are so fragile that they need glue
But they move so fast that
Now I can't see you!

In December, 1990, Sonoma State University named a room
in the Student Union in honor of Erin. Also, a scholarship for
outstanding leadership in Erin's name has been established.
The following are a portion of the remarks made by David
Farrell, Associate Dean of Student Life, for the dedication of
the Erin Fisher Room:

David Farrell: Today marks the culmination of an eighteen month
    effort by a group of students and staff to do something that
    isn't done very often at this or any other university cam-
    pus...to dedicate the name of a room in a campus building in
    the memory of a student. At this university it has only been
    done once before.

    A curious bystander would no doubt give pause to engage
    in some speculation about what incredible accomplishments
    this person named Erin had been able to do in her relatively
    short time at the university [three semesters] to warrant such
    distinction....The answer...is not to be found in what Erin did
    as a student leader on campus, the answer is found first in the

way she did things, which operationally defined the kind of person Erin was; and second, the impact her leadership experiences had on her own development...As she began attending ASP board meetings she was somewhat timid and reserved. Gradually she gained confidence, to the point that she was encouraged to assume the chair position for Fine Arts. From then on anyone even remotely associated with student life could not fail to notice the incredible growth and development of Erin. In this respect, then, we are saying that Erin's memory will always represent the best that the university experience has always offered--the development of the total person. In effect, she will be sharing something with every student that will henceforth participate in a meeting or activity in this room, the Erin Fisher room.

But as much as this dedication is for the common experiences of involved students that she represented so well, it is also for the very uncommon essence of who Erin the person was, and will always be in the memories of those who were associated with her. Everyone here today...all share deep feelings of love and affection for a sometimes quiet, oftentimes zany young lady who had somehow discovered a special secret about life at a relatively early age. A secret that developed the profound degree of love and affection for her from others; the art of giving to others....

Erin embodied the spirit of a dedicated selfless student leader. The operative term here is selfless. Always there with a beaming smile and a willingness to help everyone else, this was Erin's secret....

6-3-89
Does he know
what he means to me
Does he care
to see me again
Does he remember
our moments together
Did he save
my letters
Does he read
and feel warm inside
Does he weep
in confusion
Does he yearn
to be with me
Does he wonder
what has become of me
    I do

6-3-89
Joy is all around
Beauty is everywhere
Stop and take the time
To see
Pleasure comes from
The smallest of things
If only your thoughts permit

6-3-89
His beauty
So deep within
Can he feel it
Does he see it
The woman from which he came
Does not
Why does he seem
To only penetrate me
So deeply I feel him
Never a kiss
Never a touch
Emotions only
For years
Misunderstood by most, if not all
Perhaps himself included
Where are you
Lost boy?
Found man

6-4-89
Thinking back
Remembering the moments
Writing to keep them
As if I'd forget
Brings me pain
Fear
Handled the moments
Trouble with the memories

6-4-89. Sunday, 11:41 p.m. I just got done "tending" to the "things" on my legs. A couple of those gross little whiteheads on my legs have gotten out of hand. One in particular. It's been there about two weeks now. Started as the others—a gross bothersome little whitehead down at the bottom of my left leg. Now it's red, tender and needs to be drained of pus at least twice a day. More pus keeps coming out each day. It's not healing. Now another one on my right leg is starting to look like it wants to follow the pattern.Last night around 2 a.m., or actually I think it was closer to 3:30 or 4:00 a.m. because I had just finished my treasured book *Kismet* [We had been looking at books in a used book store and Erin had a stack of books she wanted to purchase when she discovered *Kismet*. She immediately put aside all the others and, without even opening this new find, purchased it. It was published in 1894 and was part of a series called the "No Name Series," authors unknown. Kismet means fate.] and was reading the back where they tell of the other "No Name Series" books when I began to get distressed about my leg. Anyway, I went into the bathroom, drained it, put hydrogen peroxide and that Neosporin stuff on it and came back into my room and kept looking at it. What followed is a good example of either the way I've changed my thinking—made it more positive, showing my strength—or the effects of Decadron and a Percocet I had taken around 8 p.m. I looked at my obviously infected foot and thought "Gosh, I'll probably have to get my foot amputated. This is the kind of thing that you blow off as a 'zit on the leg that got out of hand' but then it overtakes your foot and you have to get it amputated." I wasn't too disturbed with this thought and I started thinking of these new plastic parts like the wire walking girl on "Incredible Sunday." I was so accepting that I was actually thinking "better the foot than the whole leg." Then I kept reading the back of *Kismet*. Weird.

6-7-89
Fuck this shit
For all it's worth
Fuck this shit
Take all the hurt
There's too much hurt!
There's too much hurt!
I'm brain dead
Pump me up with Draino
Let's see the results
But wait,
Pop one here
Pop one there
Now let's wait and see
Oh, what they've done to me
Fuck this shit
I don't want it anymore
Fuck this shit

But I'll take it.....
'cuz this was written at a time
when my head snapped but it
just came back.

Lori: Whenever I needed someone to talk to she would always be there. She really made me feel good about myself.

Lori sent me the two letters Erin had written to her in the last weeks before her death. I am including portions of each of them. The first was on a card accompanying a "fish" pillow Erin had found for Lori, written in early June:

Dear Lori,

You should be proud of yourself because you've done a great job lately! I know this is a very stressful time for you right now with ASP, finals, your grandpa [he was also ill with cancer], etc., but you've held up GREAT so far and I know you can hang in there!

I'm giving you this surprise present not only to help you get thru' this rough time but also as a congratulations gift! 1-Congratulations on being accepted to CSUN! 2-Congratulations on getting the RA position! You'll do a great job....3-Congratulations on your special award for your hard work in ASP. I'm so glad that you were recognized because all year long you really did give it your all. Again, you should be very proud of yourself...This present is also to show you how much I appreciate the fact that you are *always* there for me. I know it's hard because I feel so different all the time and you never know what to

Knowledge of Life After Death

expect from me. I'm sorry, I really wish it wasn't like that. But it is, and I thank you for being such a truly, dear friend. I love you!

    Love,
    Erin

This letter frightened Lori as she felt that Erin knew that she was going to die. I had been somewhat alarmed myself at Erin's urgency to give the gift of the fish pillow to Lori:

Written 6-7-89:
Hi Lori!
Right now it's Wednesday night and I can't sleep. I don't know what time it is but I'm watching David Letterman and it's almost over. I'm in the upstairs room and I don't have a T.V. Guide so in a minute I'm going to have to pick my lazy butt off the couch and flip the channels (no remote control up here either—what is this world coming to?) I hope there is something decent on. Nothing scary like the *Twilight Zone!*

    I'll probably talk to you tomorrow so I was going to try to avoid writing anything that we would talk about. But then I remembered how I felt today and had a thought that I may not be taking calls tomorrow. Yesterday they left out one of my chemo drugs again so I was expecting to feel pretty good. Wrong! I feel kinda bad for Roni because all we did was lay around and watch T.V. It was really nice to see her but I felt so bad today I just wanted her to go. She left in the afternoon and I crashed on my Mom's bed until evening.

Remember how I told you I got those weird mood swings where I just start crying for no reason? Well, it happened last night when Roni was here but luckily I snuck upstairs and nobody knew I was bawling in the bathroom! It's so scary when that happens because I have no control and I don't know when they're coming. It happened tonight, too. Yukky.

How do you like my homemade stationery? I know, I know, I have this thing with palm trees. Well, they're easy to draw, what can I say?

I hope you and Michelle had fun in Sausalito. How was the weather? Did you buy anything? Ice cream, maybe? I'm hoping you picked me up a pair of hip sunglasses. Did ya, did ya? Ha Ha. Oh, oh. I feel like I'm gonna puke. Don't be alarmed. I'll end the letter now just in case. That would be going too far for homemade stationery if you get what I mean. I know it's gross—I'm sorry! No, really I'd better do something about this. I'll talk with you later.

Love,
Erin

Roni: I had a week break between college and my summer job and wanted to come see her. She wouldn't let me back out even though the day I was to come was her chemo day. We went to Chinese food, ate chocolate cake batter, and talked about how wonderful the future was going to be. It was always the next thing, not the last thing; always how great, not how awful....I left her that day, waving and smiling despite a painful cough. Three days later she was in a coma. One day after that Fish was gone. [Roni's memory has inadvertently compressed the time span.] *I wondered as she lay there if she was fright-ened or if this was just one more adventure that none of us could join. I like to think that it is the latter. I also like to think that because there weren't any horns or lights that she isn't truly gone. That she's still here to make that empty spot just a little less empty. Erin taught me that life is too special to be spent worrying about what isn't there. It should be spent appreciating what is there.*

6-10-89. It's Saturday afternoon and there's a lot of info I want to write down. This will be crucial infor-mation when I write my book.

Okay, as of last Monday my breathing problem was improving, yet not gone. I was able to walk 1/2 mile (my first walk in many days—weeks I think!) and it was my knees/legs that gave me problems not really my breathing.Tuesday morning I was get-ting ready for Roni to come. Yes, and I was getting chemo that afternoon too (which by the way was the 2nd treatment of the 3rd cycle meaning I'm halfway done!)—brave of me to have a guest! Anyway, Tuesday morning I took some laundry down and emptied the garbage and came upstairs with some laundry and was totally out of breath. Very unpre-dictable since I had walked a 1/2 mile the night before without problems. This was so bad that I was afraid that Roni would come right then and I would not be able to go downstairs to let her in (Mom was at the store)! Well as long as the breathing problem is obviously still there, I should be on the same dose of Decadron, right? Seems logical to me not to reduce the dose until the problem is completely gone and then start tapering. And there is no one that wants to start tapering off more than me but, shit, I'm not stupid.

Well, I went in for chemo Tuesday afternoon to their new "office" which turned out to be a wing of a hospital. Pretty strange. It was big but kind of sterile and industrial (echoing rooms, light bulbs hanging on wires) but they weren't done redecorating/carpeting, etc. so it will be better. The waiting room was really nice though: pretty blue carpet, and Godiva Chocolates for the patients. Of course I grabbed a chocolate. Mistake! I bit into it not knowing that there was some gooey liquid stuff inside and it came out all over me and the carpet! I squealed and looked out at the receptionist and the young, teenage one looked at me with such horror or disgust or something that I was *so* embarrassed and probably ended up making a bigger scene than if I hadn't caught her looking! Of course Donna came in right then as I'm cleaning the *new* carpet and trying to clean myself while still eating the candy and asks if I'm ready to get my blood taken. Never before had they been ready for me right when I got there but this time—of course! So I had to tell her to wait and then Mary came in and saw the whole thing, etc., etc. When I went in to get my blood taken Mary made me get on the scales. Last week 138, this week 141. I tried to laugh it off and joked that I shouldn't have had that chocolate—how embarrassing.

Now anyway back to the important part. I see Dr. Nichols and she decided that I should go down to 10 mg. of steroids a day. I told her I didn't think I should because my breathing problem is still there! She was a bitch and said that 2 mg. won't make a difference and that I'll stay at that dose for a couple of weeks so it will be okay. With much disgust I agreed and now

I'm pissed at myself for not standing up for what I know is right. Also, she looked at the infected spot on my leg. I told her I had been draining it and she snapped, "What do you mean you *have* to drain it?" I told her it hurts and fills up with pus so I put heat on it and squeeze it out. She was mad and told me not to touch it, etc., etc. "Heat is okay but don't squeeze it. You are very susceptible to infection right now. You have to be careful. We may have to drain it surgically. Call me if there's any change." Well, babe, it's quite obvious there is already an infection since it's been there at least two weeks and seems to be getting worse not better. Since then I've kept it covered w/gauze and stuff (now it's yellow, not white—Mom says green is next!) keeps coming out. At this point I'm very unhappy with Dr. Nichols, and Dr. Gold for that matter, because he has seemed to blow this breathing shit off as being "nothing serious."

So anyway, since Tuesday I was—against my will—taking 10 mg., not 12, a day. Yesterday my breathing got so bad that I could not walk from my bedroom to the bathroom without being out of breath. It continuously got worse all day to the point of me actually wanting to go into the hospital because at least then it would seem like they would be doing something to help me! A few weeks ago Maxine said she was going to have me see a lung doctor had my breathing not improved with the increased Decadron but it had so she scratched that idea. But now I'm sure when I call her Monday that that will be her next move. Makes a lot of sense since they are always telling me my lungs are completely clear! Obviously there is no lung problem. It's radia-

tion pneumonitis and a lung doctor won't know shit
about that! Needless to say I am calling Dr. Love
Monday because she is the one I trust with this. Oh,
I forgot to mention that since my breathing was so
bad last night (and still today) that I took matters
into my own hands and went back up to 12 mg.
Robert Jones just dropped by unexpectedly. I was
really embarrassed because my face is pretty big
today. Then he left and we had dinner and I have
totally lost my train of thought about what I was
writing earlier. I guess I got most of the important
stuff down.

Dear Erin,

I'm sitting here listening to U2's Achtung Baby, *more specif-*
ically "Ultra Violet (Light My Way)," and I realize you've
never had a chance to hear it. There is so much great music in
life that we've been denied the chance to share. You've never
heard Pearl Jam, Automatic for the People *or Nabby's other*
band. You've never been to Lollapalooza or The Dead. All these
musical odysseys into the human spirit that you would have
embraced.

You've never even seen my fuckin' TV show. It's just not
the same without you.

Mom and Dad used to hate rock music. Remember how
Dad used to rag on me for spending all my money on it? I was
supposed to be succumbing to broadcast television and the bor-
ing Middle Class "American Dream" instead. Remote con-
trol...cool. Would you believe that your death has caused them
to open their minds and souls to music now? They even like Bob
Marley, for God's sake! That's one good thing about your
departure, I guess, if I had to name something. It made Mom
and Dad cool.

I'm supposed to write something about what you were like.

I feel that Mom wants me to elevate you to sainthood, but, thankfully, you weren't a fuckin' saint. I keep thinking how we measured a successful party--we'd look at each other, survey the unconscious bodies on the ground, and congratulate ourselves on hitting "a new low." You were such a kind, loving person, but my most vivid memory of you was when you revealed your most violent side ("Get the fuck out!") at the Deep Throat *party. Whoa! I was so impressed.*

I'll get sappy for a minute and reminisce about how you were always willing to help others when my attitude was "fuck 'em." Remember our birthday dinner one night in San Francisco? We had just scarfed on oysters, crab and Margaritas to the point where we were gonna burst. You had a white take-out box (one of your favorite things) of leftover shellfish linguine and, while we were walking to the car, we passed a starving homeless woman with her child. We walked right by them, ignoring them...looking the other way. You were a few yards past, when you stopped and turned around and gave the woman your white box. This may sound trite on paper, but in reality, it was intense. You were the only one in the family to acknowledge the obvious social problem. It wasn't a solution, but, at least, you fed someone for the night.

But, back to music. Despite her new-found revelations, Mom is still probably wincing that I'm mentioning music so much, but it was so central to our lives, albeit, in different ways. You unknowingly summed it up best during your last New Year's Eve party '88-89. It was 2 a.m., and we were the only ones at the party who weren't passed out. You were diagnosed with Hodgkin's at this point, but you were hardly "sick."

You put on Mom and Dad's scratchy vinyl Sound of Music *soundtrack and proceeded to act out the entire Von Trapp Family saga. The music was so cheesy, but as you twirled around to* My Favorite Things *and* Edelweiss, *you brought*

*forth the essence as to what music (and life) is about--the never-
ending pursuit of everlasting love and eternal satisfaction...of
good feeling triumphing over the dark side. I'll never forget it.*

*Hmmm...I could go on forever, but I need to wrap this up.
I need to mention that how great it was that you once shared a
Domino's pizza with Jimmy Page, how you helped me meet
Paul Westerberg, how we drank all of Slayer's beer at Club
Can't Tell, and how you would truthfully tell me I was being a
shithead when others were afraid to mention it.*

*Wow. Lots of memories. Too much to put on paper. Thanks
for being around when you were. Thanks for being a friend. It's
not the same without you.*

Love, Lizz

On Monday morning, June 12, I discovered that Erin had
experienced a very difficult night. She did not awaken us
and we did not hear her coughing. Erin would not let me call
her oncologist until I attempted to get in touch with Dr. Love
who was unavailable that early. I called the oncology office
and talked to the nurse who asked if we needed an ambulance. I did not realize at this point how serious things had
become and I felt that Erin, who was ferociously indepen-
dent, would rather go in the car. I said I could get her to the
hospital. (Erin later told me she would gladly have gone in
the ambulance.) We were told to go directly to radiology and
Dr. Nichols would meet us there.

After the x-ray we were told to wait for Dr. Nichols. Erin
told a technician that she needed oxygen but was informed
that if the doctor hadn't ordered it she couldn't be given anything. We waited in radiology for nearly an hour before Dr.

Nichols arrived. The staff kept telling me the doctor would be right there, and no one seemed particularly disturbed by Erin's breathing difficulty even though at this point it was very obviously a serious situation.

When Dr. Nichols finally arrived, I greeted her with anger, telling her that this time she was going to do something, and that we were not leaving the hospital until we had some answers. But it was clear from her demeanor that something very serious was visible on the x-rays. We were sent to "admitting" and there we sat again and filled out forms and waited for an escort to come after Erin.

It took quite some time for the escort to arrive. He had come into admitting and looked for us but because Erin was dressed in a sweatsuit and a hat that covered her hair he had not realized she was the patient he had come to take to her room. I did not hear this myself but Erin later told me that she heard the escort tell a nurse that he had been looking for a girl and when he saw Erin he thought that she was a boy. That comment hurt her deeply. It should not have been made in her presence.

She was given oxygen immediately after being taken to her room and she grinned at me and said, "I knew I needed oxygen." It helped considerably.

Erin was having very severe coughing attacks at this point, similar to those she had in late April. The nurse went running to tell the doctor that Erin was having bronchospasms, after indicating to me that this was very serious.

Dr. Eagles, the pulmonary specialist who had been

called in by Dr. Nichols when Erin was admitted to the hospital, motioned for me to step out in the hall with him after he had finished examining Erin. He told me this was a life threatening situation. The nurses were not able to get a sputum sample because of the broncho-spasms so he was scheduling a lung biopsy as soon as an operating room was free.

I then had to call Erin's father at work and tell him what had been happening. Ron knew nothing of this as Erin was still in bed when he had left for work that morning. I made an attempt at staying calm on the phone but pretty much lost it when I told him what the situation was. Ron arrived in minutes as his place of business was nearby.

We then had to call Lizz and tell her of Erin's worsening condition and that she would be going into surgery soon. For whatever reason, I can't remember now, the surgery was delayed for several hours giving Lizz time to make the trip from Sacramento. I will always cherish the memory of the delighted look on Erin's face when her sister walked in the door. I was really proud of Lizz because she came in very poised and all smiles, and I knew the horror she must have been feeling but was trying so hard not to let her sister see.

Erin was terribly frightened of the upcoming surgery because she remembered how painful it was when she had her spleen removed, but she told us later that this time was different. It wasn't anything like the previous operation.

The biopsy indicated overwhelming pneumocystis carinii pneumonia, lung scarring caused by bleomycin, and radiation pneumonitis. Proper medication was now being given. We were not allowed to spend much time with Erin in Intensive Care, but she was aware of our being there and would write short notes. She was very weak and heavily medicated. She also had a tube down her throat and was on a respirator, so communication on her part was written.

On Wednesday evening, June 14, Erin's dad told her he had received a raise. She made a circle with her thumb and forefinger to indicate that she was very pleased. Ron and I went home during the night to feed the dog and to get a few hours sleep. I remember that on Thursday morning Erin indicated her pleasure at my coming to the hospital dressed in blue jeans and tennis shoes. I asked her if she wanted her cassette player and tapes and she indicated that, yes, she did. I have the little notes she wrote in the hospital, one was telling a nurse that it was O.K., another nurse had also had a problem taking her blood pressure the day before. Then Erin had requested Benadryl because she was itching all over. She had then drawn a smiley face.

Later that morning a cardiologist was called in to place an IV port in Erin's neck because the veins in her arms had collapsed. The doctor was not able to complete the procedure and the IV was put into her thigh instead. He later told Ron that he had a difficult time trying to insert the port into Erin's neck because of extensive tissue damage caused by the radiation treatment, and because of this damage he had accidently punctured the carotid artery. This procedure was done in the morning. Late that afternoon Erin had a stroke which paralyzed one side of her body. We no longer had any visible response to our being there.

Dr. Milton, who was filling in for the lung specialist that evening, told us he thought the mistake made earlier in the day had caused the stroke. The cardiologist also told us later that he thought he had caused it. He seemed very distraught. I will always appreciate his honesty.

An infectious disease specialist was called in from San Francisco as a consultant on the case. She told us that she was quite certain that Erin had had the pneumonia for quite some time and that the cortisone she was taking had masked symptoms, such as fever. (Erin had taken her temperature Sunday night, we were fanatical about that, but she did not have a fever at that time.) The specialist expressed shock at the sore on Erin's leg and told us that she thought it went all the way into the bone.

On Friday afternoon, my two sisters arrived from Oregon. I remember my sister, Linda, telling Erin that she had better get well soon as she was her best audience. Erin's face crinkled slightly as though she had heard and was trying to smile. Linda could always make her laugh. That night my sisters spent the night with Erin so Ron and I could go home for a few hours sleep.

By this time many of Erin's friends were at the hospital waiting with us, and Ron and I were trying our best to comfort them, I'm sure in part to avoid facing what was happening to our precious little girl.

Ron and I spent most of Friday talking to Erin, telling her that she needed to use her visualization technique to help out the medicine, that she had to fight. We discovered that when the nurses changed shifts they were passing on to the next shift what we were doing and they were doing the same, urging her to fight. That meant a great deal to us.

At this point we were spending most of our time around Erin's bed. We no longer asked for permission to go into Intensive Care and we were not challenged, with one exception. I can't remember if this happened on Friday or Saturday when the chaplain came to me as I stood by Erin's bed and suggested that I go into the adjoining cubicle as I was getting in the way of the nurses. I took one look at him, went right to a nurse and asked her if I was in the way. She looked startled and said, no, that if she needed me to move she would just ask me to do so and that of course I could stay near Erin. Ron then took the chaplain aside and told him that it would take an army to move me from Erin's side.

Late Saturday afternoon the doctors told us that Erin had suffered a massive stroke, and then, "poof," they all disappeared. We saw very little of her oncologist all that week and not at all when it became obvious Erin's life would soon be over. A nurse came to us and asked what we wanted done if Erin went into cardiac arrest. Should they try to save her? About this time Erin's cardiologist came in. He had not been in previously that day because it was Saturday and he was aghast at the suggestion and said that of course we should try to save her. He also said that we needed to call in another neurologist for a second opinion.

The nurse told us that since it was Saturday night it

would be difficult to find someone. But we left her no choice, we insisted. Soon after, the nurse was able to reach a Dr. Peters who came in immediately. He examined Erin and very bluntly told us that our daughter was brain dead. Dr. Peters added that he could not tell us what to do, he only knew what he would do under similar circumstances. It was obviously being left up to us to make the decision on whether Erin's life support should be disconnected, and we decided to wait until morning. Erin died at 4:15 a.m., June 18, 1989, Father's Day. Thankfully, we were spared the most agonizing decision a parent could ever have to make.

• • • •

Pneumocystis carinii pneumonia is an opportunistic disease and we were told by Dr. Eagles, the attending lung specialist, that it is common in Hodgkin's patients. It attacks immuno-suppressed persons, and Erin was definitely in this category for the following reasons. 1—Erin had Hodgkin's Disease. 2—She had undergone six weeks of radiation therapy. 3—Erin was receiving chemotherapy. 4—In addition to chemo, she was also taking cortisone which weakens the immune system.

Erin was not sent to a lung specialist. She was not given a pulmonary function test, and no sputum samples were taken. No tests for arterial gasses were given to Erin until she was admitted to the hospital on June 12. The infectious disease specialist who was called in told me that pneumocystis carinii pneumonia can be very subtle and does not necessarily show up on x-rays. (I have found substantiation of this in my research.)

Erin's death certificate showed cause of death as pneumocystis carinii pneumonia, caused by cortisone treatment for radiation pneumonitis. No mention was made of the stroke on the death certificate.

Puella Aeternus

The summer
Erin flew away
I would roller skate
Along the river
   I would sing
    She's up there
   All alone
   I'm down here
   Changing lanes
I would imagine
Erin in heaven
Scouting the seas
For whales
   My confidante
Everything natural
Fantasy and wonderment
Youth and joy
   Little Erin
   Never would have
   Grown up or old
She would have been
The Eternal Girl
   And yet
   She is.

—Wendy Cole Clark

Chapter Nine

Butterfly: It's the symbol of the pituitary glands higher telepathic power, and also the symbol of the higher intuition, symbol of reincarnation. A blessing as a disciple.

—Ann Ree Colton

The butterfly is a symbol of rebirth, or the transition from one life to another in almost every culture in the world. In the past five years we have had many interesting encounters with butterflies. Coincidence, perhaps, but perhaps not. I just know these events actually have happened. Four days after Erin's death we scattered her ashes, and when the last of them floated away in the wind, a yellow and black butterfly appeared and hovered in that area. I thought, "How beautiful." Ron went to get my sisters who had waited a short distance away in order to give us time alone to say our good-byes to Erin. When he returned with them, I told them about the butterfly which was still in the area. My sister, Linda, went down like a rock, clutching her chest. My first thought was that she was having a heart attack and I was very frightened. Then I realized that my sister, Kathy, was telling her over and over, "Tell them about the butterfly, tell them about the butterfly."

My sisters had been sharing a bedroom in our home and after they had retired the evening of Erin's passing they were discussing our decision for cremation. Linda was having difficulty accepting this decision. She said that she had visualized a bright white light, it was as though she was watching a video, and in the light was a butterfly. She did not mention this to Ron and me, but at the time she had told Kathy that if a butterfly appeared when we scattered the ashes it would mean cremation had been the correct decision. And there was the butterfly still hovering in the same area even though fifteen or twenty minutes had passed.

A "Celebration of Erin's Life" was held two days later at SSU in a natural amphitheater on campus. As I greeted arriving friends, I felt compelled to tell them that whenever they saw a yellow and black butterfly to think of Erin as it was very significant. At the time I didn't realize just how significant. We had chosen some special music to be played, and then anyone who cared to speak had the opportunity to do so and, oh my, did they do so. It was overwhelming to us as person after person, of all ages, stood up to tell his or her story about Erin. A friend of ours who had never met Erin said that she felt she really knew her after hearing all that was said that day.

The wind was very strange that morning as a breeze seemed to come up at just the appropriate times. Several people mentioned to me later that it sounded like applause as it rustled the leaves in the trees surrounding the amphitheater. I even mentioned to Ron during the service to listen to the wind.

During the service something was said that brought to my mind a conversation Erin and I had several months prior. We had heard an owl and I told her that one of my favorite books is *I Heard the Owl Call My Name*. It is about a young priest who has a terminal disease. He is sent to live in an Indian village in Alaska and while there learns their customs and beliefs. One belief was that when it was time for them to leave this earth they would hear an owl call their name, and for some reason during Erin's service this thought came into my mind.

That evening after our family and friends had left, Ron and I were sitting in the living room watching for the deer Erin loved so much to make their nightly trek across the driveway. An owl flew up and landed on the street lamp near the house and remained there until it was too dark to see it anymore. (This type of meaningful coincidence is known as synchronicity.)

Just as the service concluded and we stood, my sister, Kathy, excitedly grabbed my arm, pointed, and exclaimed,

"Look at the butterfly. Look at the butterfly." There it was, a huge black and yellow butterfly flying in a straight line down the hill into the amphitheater. It flew back and forth over the seats and then away. The timing could not have been more perfect if planned. Several days later my brother asked, "Who released the butterfly?" Was it coincidence that the butterfly appeared? Perhaps.

Our daughter, Lizz, lives in a large city, not where one would expect to see many butterflies, but in the following three weeks after Erin's death Lizz was literally dive-bombed by a yellow and black butterfly on two different occasions. In each instance it flew straight at her and she could feel the flutter of its wings in her hair.

At approximately this same time I recall walking back from picking up the mail (we lived in the country and had to walk a short distance to the main road to the mailbox) and looking at information sent to us by "The Compassionate Friends," a bereavement support group for those who have lost children, and being somewhat taken aback by the symbol used on their literature—a butterfly. I then looked up and at arm's length was a yellow and black butterfly. It was so close I could have reached out and touched it. Again, a very meaningful coincidence.

I also remember falling to pieces one morning and going out into the back yard sobbing uncontrollably, and there again was the butterfly. It hovered close by for quite some time and then flew to the living room window and then away.

Several weeks later one of Erin's friends, Robert Jones, dropped by to visit and to return the tape containing the music we had chosen for the service. While we sat in the backyard talking, a huge yellow/black butterfly floated through the yard, flew quite close to the three of us and then away. I might add that Robert was a very special friend. He had visited Erin many times when she was hospitalized and would sit quietly beside her lending his support. He would drop by the house from time to time to see how she was doing, often bringing a red rose for her.

In another instance, a long time friend stopped by to see us when he was in the area for business reasons. Erin had been flower girl at his wedding when she was a youngster and they had a very special relationship. We walked out onto the back deck and a yellow/black butterfly was right there, so close it startled us. I still remember the mixture of astonishment and wonder on his face. (He was at the service and knew the "butterfly" story.)

On Father's Day, 1990, we went up on Mt. Tamalpais as this was a very sacred, special mountain to Erin. She went there seeking peace and comfort when she was feeling down, and we also like to go there from time to time. Ron wandered down the trail to be by himself for a few minutes and I remember sitting on a rock wondering whether we would see a butterfly, and then there it was, just doing butterfly things, flitting from flower to flower. Then it did something quite unusual for a butterfly. As Ron turned and started back up the trail to join me, the butterfly flew straight to him and then around his body in a close circle. He could have easily reached out and touched it. (This day was also the 1st anniversary of Erin's death.)

About this same time period another of Erin's friends had come to spend the afternoon with me and as we sat in the living room talking I looked up just as a butterfly "looked" in the window. It was not just flying by, it was facing towards the window, hovering. I did not point it out to the friend as he was not aware of the previous happenings with the butterfly.

In the late summer of 1990, Ron and I went to Oregon to spend a week with my family. We had gone kayaking with my sister and her husband and as the men were loading the kayaks back onto the car a yellow/black butterfly hovered nearby until we drove away. It stayed for 20-30 minutes.

In May, 1991, three days prior to our trip to New York to see George Anderson (this trip will be explained in a following chapter) while I was taking our dog, Bridget, for her daily walk I had another strange experience with a butterfly. This time it was a small orange and black one that accompanied the dog and me. As we were slowly meandering up the hill at a snail's pace (a Basset Hound has to smell every twig and bug), a butterfly landed at our feet and then flew four or five feet ahead and then again sat on the sidewalk. It stayed there until we came so close that I was afraid the dog would step on it. Then the butterfly again flew four or five feet and landed on the sidewalk. It continued to do this all the way up the hill and even followed the curve of the sidewalk as it turned near the top. I remember going back to the house and telling Ron that a butterfly had literally taken a walk with us. This gave me a great deal of pleasure but I did not attribute any meaning to it until it happened again several days later on the morning we were to leave for New York and in exactly the same way.

Along the sidewalk there were wildflowers and dry grasses where a butterfly could light. But this butterfly again chose to sit on the sidewalk as we approached. It waited until we had reached that point and then flew a few feet ahead. We all continued up the hill in the identical way we had done previously—Helen, Bridget and the butterfly. It was a delightful happening for me regardless of whether any special significance was intended.

Soon after our return from New York, a friend came by the house to hear the tape we had made of our visit to George Anderson. She had recently lost her child, also. After hearing the recording she stated that she believed that we had contacted Erin but informed me that the *Bible* says we are not to contact those who have died. My retort was that this was all so beautiful with the butterfly, etc., how could it possibly be wrong. I then glanced out the window and there was a huge yellow/black butterfly very close by. My friend nearly fell off her chair when I pointed it out to her. Again, wonderful timing on the part of a butterfly.

In August, 1991, Erin's good friend, Erinn Nabong, was married, eloped actually, and soon after that she and her new husband were walking from their car to their apartment when a yellow/black butterfly circled the new bridegroom, adding another to the growing list of coincidences.

In the fall of 1991, Erin's cousin, Robbie, started his first year at a college on the East Coast and he was experiencing the usual pangs of loneliness associated with being away from home for the first time. Home for Robbie was in Oregon, many miles away. In October, on the day of his birthday, he was really feeling depressed and homesick, a very down day for him. Robbie was on campus talking to a friend when a yellow/black butterfly landed on his friend's shoulder and proceeded to sit there for quite a long time. This was the only time Robbie saw a butterfly that fall. I also must add that he and Erin had a very close relationship. After a visit to our house in the fall of '88, Robbie told his mother that Erin was one of the nicest persons he had ever known.

In June, 1992, another close friend, Lori Fish, was married. This was a very difficult occasion for Ron and me to attend as Erin would have been in the wedding party but we also realized how much it would mean to Lori for us to be there and, without a doubt, Erin would have expected us to attend. It was a beautiful garden wedding and I kept looking for a butterfly but none appeared during the ceremony, butterfly but none appeared during the ceremony, but as we were leaving there it was, hovering near our car. Only this time there were two butterflies doing what might have been a mating ritual—they were hovering and fluttering in a way we had never seen before. Everyone returning to their cars noticed and commented on the butterflies. Several months later I mentioned this to Lori and she said, yes, that the butterflies were there all day and were very close by when pictures were taken after the ceremony.

In late July, 1992, Lizz, Ron and I were going out to dinner to celebrate Lizz's birthday and as we were walking from her house to the car there again was our yellow/black butterfly. It flew directly at us and came very close to touching Ron as it fluttered by.

One Sunday just prior to this Ron and I had gone on a picnic with some close friends. They had reserved a wonderful picnic site at a winery; it was a tiny island in a small lake with a foot bridge that crossed over to the island. On the island there was a gazebo with a table and benches, also a small grassy area with trees along the water. A very peaceful, delightful spot. Soon after we arrived, a butterfly (black/yellow, of course) flew through the gazebo very close to us and again, as has happened before, nearly touched Ron as it passed.

Later, as we were saying our goodbyes to our friends in the parking lot, one of the women noticed a beautiful rose and commented on it being there as this particular variety of rose is considered very fragile and is rarely a part of parking lot landscaping. It was a Sterling Silver, a lavender rose.

This variety of rose held a special significance for me because of an event which occurred earlier that same week. Prior to this event I had never heard of a Sterling Silver Rose. I will write of this in a later chapter.

When Ron joined me I took him to see the rose and the butterfly chose that moment to put in another appearance.

In August, 1992, we had very close family visiting us, my sister and her two daughters and a very special nephew and his family. We had just gotten into the swimming pool when a yellow/black butterfly swooped down over the length of the pool, after first coming within a fraction of an inch of touching Ron's hair.

The next month Ron, Lizz and I spent a Sunday at "Ala Carte in the Park" in Golden Gate Park in San Francisco. We had a very pleasant day wandering from booth to booth tasting all types of food. Late in the day we took our plates and went to sit on a grassy hillside to eat. As we were trying to get arranged, along came a yellow/black butterfly and, as always, it flew right in Ron's face and then away. It did not come close to any others sitting on the hillside.

While vacationing in Santa Fe, New Mexico, Ron and I were going through art galleries on a street called Canyon Road. This is a lovely street and various trees were in full blossom, a very beautiful setting. Yes, our butterfly was there.

Later that evening while lying in bed, I said silently to Erin that we were going back to Canyon Road the following day and that if she was with us to prove it by having the butterfly appear again. The next afternoon, just as we exited our car, there it was. It came swooping down upon us and, as so many of them have done before, came very close to Ron. What a beautiful picture it made as it fluttered past the burst of pink of a blossoming tree.

The next month two of my nephews were visiting us and they wanted to go to an amusement park where they had gone with Erin many times. As they left for the park that morning I had a very strong feeling that the butterfly would put in an appearance that day, so I told them to look for it. It was there. My nephew said that when they entered the park he knew where he would see the butterfly—at a ride called The Revolution where he and Erin had such fun in 1988 when the two families had gone together for the day, and he was correct. While he was standing watching the ride, a yellow and black butterfly flew close by him at eye level. He could not have missed it.

This concludes our experiences with butterflies but I have one additional bit of information to add. At some time in the past five years I read or was told that the children standing in line for the gas chambers in Nazi Germany during World War II used their fingernails to scratch pictures of butterflies on the walls while they waited to enter the gas chambers. I have since found verification of this in *On Children and Death* by Elisabeth Kübler-Ross.

Soar

Life is a strand,
    a beautiful strand of beads.
As every day passes,
    a new bead is placed on this strand.
Only the maker of this strand,
    can decide how big or beautiful each bead is.
Each bead reflects beauty and feeling,
        the beauty of the day it represents.

And when the heart stops beating,
    the necklace is complete.
This strand of pure life,
    is now placed around the neck of the spirit.
This spirit,
    is the spirit that drove the now still heart.
This spirit,
    is the spirit that felt the necklace becoming
    complete.
And now, in a beautiful joining called death,
    the necklace and the spirit, become one.

And on the day of your joining,
    a prophet was born.
An infant with infinite wisdom,
    whose eyes glittered with your beauty.

And on the day of your joining,
  the Grand Canyon smiled with hope.
It laughed at our small problems,
  and reassured the world with your solace.

And on the day of your joining,
  the homeless felt at home.
Over the blue water,
  and under the blue sky.

This day,
  so sorrowful on the surface.
Yet, so magnificent deep down.
Say not, "what a terrible day,"
  say unto yourself, "I love more, now."

I recognize the butterfly,
  not as an insect.
But, a symbol of simple beauty.
A symbol of inner freedom.

Freedom to stand with arms wide,
  in front of an oceanside sunset.
Freedom to breathe crisp mountain air
  and sing a song of life.

I recognize the butterfly,
  not just as a being.
But, a being of beauty.
Whose wings blanket me while I sleep.

Beauty as pure as April rain.
Beauty as soft as a newborn's velvet skin.

This butterfly, this free soul,
I love it so.
Come to me in the rain,
I shall shelter you.
Come to me in the darkness,
   and I shall offer my inner candle.
My candle, the candle that burnt brighter,
   on the day of your joining.

And on the days that followed your joining,
   the spirits danced on the mountaintop.
The wind blowing, the grass swaying.
They danced an African dance,
   in a circle around and around.
In the middle of this circle,
   appeared your spirit wearing your necklace.
Your spirits' arms were spread wide,
   encompassing the bay-area splendor.

Then the butterflies joined in,
   fluttering and spinning,
   while your spirits danced with smiles.

During this dance,
   all around the world,
   spirits sang a song of pureness,
   a song of exhilaration.

The clouds bounced to and fro,
  their arms enlocked with a wink.
It rained on Kenyan ground,
  and snow fell all around me,
  blanketing my naked shoulders.
Every crystal different,
  as is every life on this world.

Each crystal follows its own path,
  its own destiny determined by the sky.
They fall without worry, being happy,
  knowing they would all hit the
  all-engulfing ground.
People are the snowflakes of life.
They resist the wind,
  while cursing their every shift.
Yet, you in your brief stay,
  sang on your way down.

Derek Clark, Age 16
(Erin's cousin)

Chapter Ten

*A*fter Erin's death I walked in a fog with this giant, gaping hole in my being. I functioned in a sense, meals were cooked, groceries bought, the house cleaned, social functions attended, all done on automatic pilot. I remember sitting on the bed many mornings saying to myself, "How do I make it through this day?" and feeling as though I too had died. Only other bereaved parents will be able to totally relate to this statement as the loss of a child is the ultimate of losses.

A friend suggested that I read some of the books about Edgar Cayce and after many months I decided to at least give it a try. I was still so numb with grief they did not help too much but they did open up another avenue of thought and I continued to bring home stacks of books from the library dealing with life after death. Some helped, but because my pain was still so great, most did not.

I had never believed in life after death and considered myself an agnostic as I could not accept the dogma that goes along with the mainstream concept of religion. I had, however, always felt a oneness with nature and believed, as the Native Americans believe, that nature has to be respected and that all life is connected in some way as a whole, but I honestly had not spent a great deal of thought on this subject.

Then one day I stumbled upon Joel Martin and Patricia Romanowski's book, *We Don't Die*, a book about psychic medium, George Anderson. George lived in Long Island, N.Y., and I knew upon finishing the book that I would meet with him. How, I wasn't sure, I just knew it would happen. This was something I had to do.

I called the cable TV station where Joel Martin worked and was given George's phone number. Ah, I thought, this will be easy. What I reached was a recording stating that all appointments were filled for the balance of 1990 (this was late summer). Logic finally prevailed and I told myself this was ridiculous, he was on the East Coast and I was on the West Coast, what a crazy idea. But I still couldn't shake the feeling that I had to see him. It was almost a feeling of a hand in the middle of my back pushing me, an intense feeling, impossible to adequately describe.

Ron at that time had not read the book and I am certain he thought I was losing my mind. But he said that if I felt so strongly about this I should try to set up an appointment, but he did not want to go. I had a friend who had lost her son the previous summer and she was eager to accompany me.

In early 1991, I attempted again to contact George. At this time people could call for an appointment only on the first Tuesday of each month and only during a two hour time span. I would sit at the phone and dial, receive a busy signal and keep dialing again and again. I usually did get through to George's secretary but his available appointments never seemed to coincide with when my friend and I could go. In March I couldn't get through at all and was getting very discouraged.

In April, I finally made the connection, well past the time calls were supposed to be taken and after more than three hours of dialing. Just as they answered Ron came home from work and said to take any appointment I could get; if my friend couldn't go at that time, he would. He knew how important this had become to me.

It would be May 15, just six weeks to wait. I was so excited. My friend was not home so I left word on her answering machine, and I knew that May 15 was a time she could get away from her job so everything seemed to be set. Ron was relieved he would not have to go.

The next morning my friend called and said in a panicky voice that she had changed her mind, she would not go with me. I was very upset with her, after all, we had discussed this at great length and she had been as eager as I to go. She said she couldn't explain, but it was almost like a crushing weight on her chest holding her back. She absolutely was not going.

The direct result of her changing her mind so abruptly was that Ron did go with me to meet with George. It was very important that he and I be there together. What was experienced that evening was meant to be shared by the two of us.

We met with George for a group session with seventeen or eighteen other people. He asked only our first names, as had been done on the phone when I called for the appointment, and he did not want to know whom we hoped to contact. George warned the group at the beginning of the evening that he could make no promises as to whom would come through to him and gave anyone who chose to leave the opportunity to do so and they would not be charged. (I must add that his fee is nominal, to say the least.)

He talked to us fairly early in the session, but we stayed the balance of the evening because what was coming through to George was absolutely fascinating and, from the reactions of the others in the group, he was as correct with them as he was with us:

George: (As he approached us) They're taking their time, too. It's like Monday I couldn't keep up with them. Tonight they're crabby. Talk faster. She tells me to tell them they're from New York, talk faster. There is a strong, there is a strong female presence here. Are you husband and wife?

Ron: Yes.

George: Did a female close to you pass over?

Ron and Helen: Yes.

George: It's like she is right here. She's standing between the two of you so I'm assuming you're husband and wife because she comes to both of you.

Ron and Helen: Yes.

George: She is family?

Helen: Yes.

George: Not that she is playing favorites, but very close to you? (Indicates Helen)

Helen: Yes.

George: (To Ron) Not that she's not glad to see you either, it's just that there must be a need that she does that, so we'll just leave it with you. There's also a male, there's two males with her as well. The female passes young?

Helen: Yes.

George: There's an older male with her. Did your Dad pass?

Ron: Yes.

George: O.K. Because she keeps saying your father is with her. They'd be related, too? Correct? O.K. (He tilts his head and looks away from us) Who do you mean to? Do you mean to these people? Your daughter passed?

Ron and Helen: Yes.

George: She keeps saying, "I'm the daughter, I'm the daughter." I'm like, do you mean to these people? And she said, "Yes." I said O.K. Sometimes it takes me a few minutes to hear this signal and get affirmed. Oh. O.K., that's right because she just said she referred to your father as her grandfather, so, well it could be your niece and that could be your grandfather but in any case we won't argue with her. (Long pause) O.K. She passes tragically, in a sense of age, I think. She talks about passing tragically in a sense of age.

Helen: Yes.

George: Obviously young when she passes over. She knew she was going to pass on? She tells me she's not shocked by death.

Helen: I think she knew.

George: O.K., because she says to me, "I'm not shocked I die, I'm not shocked by death." Even though she's not dead, she tells me she's not shocked by it. O.K. O.K. For whatever reason, she thanks you both for being good to her prior to her passing. Does it make sense?

Ron and Helen: Yes.

George: O.K. As long as you understand because she said to me, "No, just say it, just say it." I said O.K., all right. Now she singularizes herself, is she your only daughter?

Helen: No.

George: Is she the youngest or something?

Ron: Yes.

George: O.K., O.K. She keeps talking, as she stands there she makes me feel she's singularizing herself and that is usually a clue for something like she's the only child, the youngest or something like that. Which is another reason this hits home, this is your youngest child, or youngest daughter. [Not having lost a child, George is perhaps not aware of the fact that it does not matter whether it is your youngest, oldest or middle child, or if you have ten other children. The grief is horrendous. The sense of loss would be just as extreme for us if it had been Lizz who had passed.] She claims she had trouble with her health, is that true?

Ron and Helen: Yes.

George: She had to live with it though?

Helen: Yes.

George: Because it seems like it's not (snaps fingers), she goes like this. She lives with it or lingers for a period of time. She goes off into a sleep at the end. Like in a coma or something?

Helen: Yes.

George: Because again, I guess you were there because she wants to tell you she knows you were there even though she might not have been able to verbally convey that message. She knows you were there, and she goes off into a sleep and then I see a vision of St. Joseph which means a happy death. She also suffers in silence a great deal?

Ron: Yes.

George: Courageously.

Helen: Yes.

George: You know, because she says I am victorious over death. You know, like she knew she was going to lick this whatever it was and she says, "I have, I'm back to my old self again. The body has died but I haven't." And definitely, if there was life after death you'd hear from her. She's got that type of a personality.

Ron and Helen: (Chuckle in agreement)

George: She left her example of strength behind, and courage, in her struggles with this. Did this affect her breathing?

Ron and Helen: Yes.

George: I feel like I can't breathe. Again, no matter what, she still tried to keep a smile on her face.

Helen: Yes.

George: "Oh, I'm fine," you know, "I'm feeling better," even though inside—.

George: (To Ron) Do you feel kind of left out with her passing? She wants you to know that she loves you and is very close to you. You might feel a sense of a kind of emptiness since she passed on. I'm sure you're not thrilled but the thing is she wants to let you know that she is very close to you.

George: (To Helen) You and she had a good mother-daughter relationship and you were also good friends?

Helen: Yes.

George: Which is the reason why she pointed to you at first but she certainly doesn't want you [Ron] to feel bad about that. You and she are close in your own way, also. And, of course, she says you are suffering within, so that's why she pulls that out. You have other children, I guess?

Ron and Helen: Yes.

George: Wait a minute, she—. Are there two others?

Ron: Yes.

Helen: In a sense. [We lost our first child, a son, due to a miscarriage.]

George: She talks about two others. And, you know, it's funny, I was going to say to you is one kind of like a brother-sister, but not? But she talks about two other siblings. Did any of this affect her chest area?

Helen: Yes, it did.

George: The troubles all up here? [Indicated chest.]

Helen: Yes.

George: Did she have anything like asthma, or does it feel like that because of the breathing trouble? Probably feels like that, O.K., because I feel like my lungs are tightening up. Did they also fill? It seems like one was worse than the other.

Helen: Probably.

George: She had trouble more so with one or this constant problem with one. Also, her heart is weakened?

Helen: Not that we know of.

George: O.K., she claims her heart is weakened even though I don't say I have trouble there but it could have been in connection with the filled—. Did it affect the blood? Was there anything wrong with the blood cells?

Helen: At the end.

George: It seems like the blood cells are going crazy.

Helen: At the end.

George: O.K. Also her eye is bothered. She's telling me her eyes are fine. Unless she had any problems that would have affected the head.

Helen: There was.

George: Because there is pressure all up here. There might have been pressure around the eye or it might have caused a strain. Also at times she might have like dizzy spells or fainting spells or something. I don't feel like I'm not getting enough oxygen to the brain. Something's faltering up here because she had pressure on the head?

Helen: Yes.

George: Because of this pressure in the head, things signal, things are faltering or something.

Helen: That makes sense.

George: Something affects the brain?

Helen: Yes.

George: Because definitely something is pushing on my brain. I've had the brain wave test, I know I have one. It has to make sense. Yeah, but once whenever this starts then I get the breathing trouble. You know the signals coming into the body are thrown off. Of course, the brain is the headquarters.   Did you talk about life after death with her or something?

Helen: A little.

George: Yes, it's almost like there was a promise made, you'll hear from me somehow. Or that somehow she would let you know she was all right.

Helen: She did make, I don't know how much I should tell you.

George: Don't tell me anything. As long as you understand, that's all that matters. This way she has more to say. I want to leave it at that.

Erin and her sister had discussed life after death and had made a promise to each other that whoever died first would contact the other if there really was an afterlife. Lizz had told me she had asked Erin to let us know, but at the time we met with George I thought she had talked to her sister when Erin was in the hospital, unconscious. Upon our return home I learned that this was a conversation which had taken place several months prior to Erin's hospitalization:

George: Did she have like a tumor?

Helen: No.

George: Anything on the brain?

Helen: Something about the brain but not—.

George: Something popped over here?

Ron: Yes.

George: Like an aneurysm or —.

Helen: Yes.

George: It felt like something pressing on the brain.

Helen: Yes.

George: *Like* a tumor?

Helen: Yes.

George: But when you said no, I said, "No, no, it's still there," and then all of a sudden it burst, it popped in my head and I said, "Well maybe that's an aneurysm or a blood clot or something of that nature." It's funny because she might have had it for awhile but didn't know it. Might have been trouble and she didn't know. You know, get a headache and take a couple of aspirin and it goes away, that sort of thing. But again, she brings up that discussion about something to do with life after death and that you'd hear from her. You've dreamed about her also? She claims she's come in dreams.

Helen: She has come in dreams, to others.

George: O.K. She says she's come in dreams.

Helen: Yes.

George: And I thought she just meant you, but it could be some other people because like she says, "I have come in dreams," so this is like a reassurance of what you've already heard, or expected.

Several months after Erin's death I heard her voice call out, "Mom." It was devastating at the time to awaken and find it was only a dream but after meeting with George I realized perhaps it wasn't such an ordinary dream after all:

George: Very creative individual? There are all colors around her. That can mean somebody that is—.

Helen: Somewhat.

George: I'm not saying she was a Leonardo Da Vinci but definitely had—she was a vibrant person, maybe that's the way to put it.

Helen: Yes, very.

George: Was she very attracted to the color lilac?

Ron and Helen: Yes. (laughter)

Erin loved purple, every shade of purple. When she was much younger we dyed every white garment that she owned varying shades of purple: tennis shoes, socks, T-shirts, hats, bras:

George: I see her appearing in front of you in lilac?

Helen: Yes. (laughing)

George: It looks like she's in a lilac dress. Did she have her hair cut? Does she wear it kind of short?

Helen: Yes.

George: Short, but feminine.

Ron and Helen: Yes.

George: She doesn't have it down to here.

Helen: Yes, it was short.

George: There's a young female in front of you that looks like she's in a lilac gown or dress and the hair is cut, you know, short by the period of the time, for this stage of today. Do you have a son? Was she seeing somebody at the time?

Helen: How much do I elaborate?

George: There's a male she talks about. Somebody she was very close with before she passed on and, you know, it could have been like a brother, or it could have been someone she had been dating, or a friend like a brother, or something like that.

Ron: Yes.

George: She seems to bring somebody up that she calls out

to. Who's Ron?

Ron: I am.

George: Oh. Is there a Ron passed on also?

Ron: No.

George: I hear her calling to Ron, so obviously she's calling to you.

We think she was indicating her friend, Roni Jones, as there would be no reason to refer to her father as anything other than Dad. Nothing further was related to Ron from her at this time, and George immediately addressed me after the reference to Ron:

George: (To Helen) That same thing, she says she was exceptionally close to you on Sunday for obvious reasons, knowing what Sunday represents [Mother's Day].

Helen: Yes.

George: She also has a sister, too?

Helen: Yes.

George: She's obviously close.

Helen: Yes.

George: Like good friends? She calls her her best friend and she said, "That's my sister." She brings that out as well. Ummm. Does the name Kim mean anything to you?

Helen: Yes.

George: Passed on?

Helen: No, living.

George: She knows her.

Helen: Yes.

George: She's asking how Kimmie is, or Kim is. Is this a friend of hers or something?

Helen: Yes.

George: "Tell her you've heard from me." They seem to have been pretty good friends. "Tell Kim you've heard from me. Also Lori?"

Helen: Yes.

George: Again, "Tell Kim, tell Lori, you've heard from me." She also talks about Pammy or Tammy or something. I can't—I'm going to drop it, I can't make out what it is. I'm not correct.

Kim is a very good friend from junior high and high school days. They had continued to be close. I called Kim and asked if her mom called her Kimmie as I had never heard her referred to as such. She laughed and said, yes, and so had Erin. Lori was Erin's roommate at college and also a very close friend. Lori had previously mentioned to me that Erin always said that Lizz was her best friend. Both of these young women are quoted in earlier chapters:

George: (To Helen) Your dad gone over?

Helen: No.

George: Grandfather, I take it?

Helen: Yes.

George: Because there's a grandfather figure with her from your side of the family. I just figured it might be your dad because she talks about her grandfather. Also, has your mom passed?

Ron: Yes.

George: (To Helen) Yours is still living?

Helen: Yes.

George: That's what it is. She tells me there's a set of grandparents with her, but your side [Ron], your mother and father. Your father feels he could have been a little closer to you, is that true?

Ron: Yes.

Ron's parents gave him and his sister to their grandparents when he was two years old. It was a very difficult life for him:

George: 'Cause he kind of, he apologizes. It's an overdue apology, he says. Not the type of man to admit he was wrong here, so he says he apologizes. He feels he abandoned you emotionally. He's there, but he's not, but he says he's been given an ample opportunity to correct that by taking good care of your daughter in the next stage, or, as he puts it, "Maybe it's the other way around, she's taking good care of me," because he welcomed her over. Then he says she's made a great influence in his life in the next stage to help him understand where his short comings were and he says so, and he doesn't mean this to be harsh, but he says, "Your loss is my gain in a spiritual sense." In the short time your daughter was here she sure has a lot of wisdom and experience.

George: (To Ron) You came from a difficult upbringing?

Ron: Yes.

George: Both parents feel things could have been happier. You're caught, you're a victim of circumstances they say, and both your parents feel they could have been closer to you. But your mother did kind of have a hard life, now within emotionally, a hard life. Her and your father have settled their differences and they're together in the next stage. Does the name Lizz mean anything at all?

Helen: Yes.

George: Passed on?

Helen: No.

George: Your daughter knows her?

Helen: Yes.

George: She's asking how Lizz is?

Ron: It's her sister.

George: Oh, O.K., she keeps calling out to Lizz. It's funny, she said, "My best friend."

Helen: Yes.

George: I was going to say, is that her best friend? Then I just realized before she referred to her sister as her best friend. She must have picked up my grouchiness in my mind. I said, "Yeah, if you could really call out to her you'd call out to her by name," and she just did. Lizz is also being congratulated. Is she graduating or something?

Helen: No.

George: Hear of happy news that affects her personally, there is congratulations around her. I won't argue with your daughter. I'll leave it with you.

Helen: That makes sense.

George: "Tell Lizz you've heard from me." She says your daughter was there for her all the time. She feels very close with her. She just wants to let her know she appreciated her love and devotion prior to her passing and— your daughter is old enough to understand this, yes?

Helen: Yes.

George: Oh, good. She's like pretty insistent you tell Lizz you've heard from her.

George: (To Ron) Hmmm. Do you have a little trouble with your health?

Ron: No.

George: Do you have any trouble with your blood pressure or anything?

Ron: No.

George: Just told to watch your health that could be set off by stress, or emotional upset that you lock in. Your father says you're like him, you keep things to yourself and keep things in. That's why your daughter brought that up before. And it doesn't mean you're having a heart attack tomorrow, what it means is you just keep alert. If you honestly don't feel right, not to hesitate to get checked. You're employed, I take it. Yes?

Ron: Yes.

George: There's also a change within your job. Are you kind of self-employed?

Ron: No.

George: Do you have control on the job?

Ron: Yes.

George: O.K., because there's a move or a change within a job but you're in control of it. That's what made me think you're self-employed; you're in control of the job, so that could be like raise, promotion, because you retire from an aspect of your work and go into something else but still connected with it. Now I'm not saying you're retiring. Ummm—you're vice-president, you retire from that and become president. That's what I'm saying. You retire from one aspect but move on into another direction.

Ron was transferred less than three months from the time we met with George. His title is the same but the total sales volume done by his new store is 2 1/2 times greater than before:

George: Is there also Mary or Marie?

Helen: My middle name is Marie.

George: (To Helen) Anybody passed on because that's why I'm looking to you, it seems to be more your side of the family. Could have been an aunt or something in the background.

Helen: I can't recall.

Upon arriving home, I checked with my father and there was a distant aunt named Mary Alameda Bowman. I had known of her only as "Aunt Allie" not realizing that her name was Mary:

George: There's also a Patty, too. Friends of your daughter, or anything?

Helen: I have a sister-in-law named Patty.

George: Are you friends with her? It seems more of a friend-ship?

Helen: Not real friends.

George: All right, let me just drop it. Could be someone—. Was she on a team?

Helen: No, not a team.

George: Would she have belonged to a club or something?

Ron and Helen: Yes.

George: 'Cause she was singularizing herself in school like someone who was on a team or belonged to a club.

Helen: Yes.

George: An extracurricular activity?

Ron and Helen: Yes.

George: O.K. She might know this person from there in that connection because she talks about being in a club.

Helen: It seems to ring a bell but I can't bring it out.

George: Yeah, that's why I said I'll leave it with you. As I said at the beginning of the night, that happens, you just can't think on the moment.

Helen: I do know who Patty is. I do remember. [This proved to be incorrect.]

George: She's calling out and I said, O.K., I'll leave it with you. She's been pretty sharp so far but she leaves it go. (To Helen) Do you have trouble with your hearing?

Helen: Just a little.

George: She's telling you to keep alert to your hearing. You certainly don't seem like you're having trouble hearing me so I was a little puzzled by that.

Helen: When there's a lot of noise.

George: Do you have like nerve damage back there [indicated right upper back] or something?

Helen: I have a back problem up in my upper back.

George: Yeah, something. I feel like a nerve is pinched back there.

Helen: That might be it.

George: Unfortunately, it seems like you have to live with it.

Helen: Great!

George: You can go to a chiropractor, have it adjusted, but I feel it always returns. Something's pinching back here and it's not causing terrible pain but it's making itself known that it's there. But it could at times affect your hearing. You might get a ringing in your ears at times. It goes away but it's no big deal but....Did you injure yourself back here, or something?

Helen: I've had back problems for years. [I have been seeing chiropractors for years.]

George: It's like it never healed back right. Something you have to live with. Something you just can't pinpoint. Watch how you sleep, though. Make sure you don't lie in awkward positions, like on your stomach.

Helen: I don't ever sleep on my stomach.

George: Yeah, you can't. You'll twist back here too much

and there's slight pressure there to begin with. Ummm, did I say Lizz was—didn't she say something about her being congratulated.

Helen: Yes.

George: O.K., because it's coming up again. She brings up hearing of happy news with her, but again it affects her as an individual like with her career or something of this nature.

Helen: There has been something that Erin would have— that she would have been proud of.

George: O.K., because she says she brings it up like there's some sort of news of congratulations with her that affects her as a person. Could be something at school, job, career, whatever, that she brings up.

Lizz had just moved into her own condominium. She also was producing and hosting a show on cable access television:

George: Also the name Julie, do you know Julie?

Ron: Yes.

George: Anyone your daughter knows.

Ron: Yes.

George: Young person?

Helen: Yes.

George: Is she family?

Helen: No.

George: Like, maybe?

Helen: No.

George: Because there seems to be a definite closeness with her. Because I'm getting the same thing with the message of congratulations with her.

At this time we thought Julie must be a neighbor of ours when Erin was in high school since she was the only Julie we were aware of at that point. Upon our return home, I was visiting with a friend of Erin's, Wendy Cole Clark, and she happened to mention that her mom's name is Julie. I asked Wendy if her mother had been given a promotion or had a change of employment recently and she said yes, that she was starting a new teaching job in the fall. She also told me how devastated her mother was over Erin's death. Ron and I are both quite certain this is the correct Julie. The only other Julie we knew just didn't seem to be appropriate as Erin had not communicated with her since we moved in 1986:

George: Is there like an aneurysm in the head? Or something like that?

Ron and Helen: Yes.

George: 'Cause again, I feel something—that's where the blood comes from. Some could have gone up there and clotted or lodged and finally the pressure can break. Was she on life support?

Helen: Yes.

George: Was she disconnected?

Helen: No.

George: Because she's glad she passes on before that would
   happen.

Helen: Yes.

George: O.K., because I see her on life support and then like
   she passed on and they, of course, disconnected it. But
   she's glad, because she didn't want to have you have to
   make that decision because it's obvious she wasn't going
   to come back, and as she said to me, "I was not coming
   back into the body if I was going to be a vegetable the
   rest of my life." She's not that type of person, she's too
   vibrant.

Ron and Helen: Yes.

George: And as parents you wouldn't want to see that anyway. So she says when she was kind of, and I don't mean
   this in a theological sense, but when she was in limbo
   deciding, "Do I stay or go," you know, caught between
   the two worlds, she made the decision. It's like she was
   talking to your parents and they explained, "This has to
   be your decision," and she decided, "O.K., I'll let go,
   because if I don't they're going to have to be forced into
   a cataclysmic decision of having to decide whether or
   not they should pull the life support and," she says, "I
   don't want to see them go through that," so she withdrew. Because she realized what an agonizing experience, I'm sure, that would have been for the two of you.
   So she says she made the decision to let go, so now you
   know she is fine and at peace. But she knows you were
   with her when she passed on. Like she knows you were
   there night and day and know she appreciates it. And
   don't feel that you should have done more for her

because she says, "Just because you are parents doesn't make you infallible, that you did as best as you could do and to this point of this problem now there was only so much you could do anyway."

Approximately eighteen months after Erin's death one of her friends came to me and said she needed to tell me about something that had happened during the time Erin was in the hospital. She is a very serious young woman and in her relating this event to me I could easily tell what an intense impression it had made on her. During the last days of Erin's hospital confinement, this young woman could sense Erin trying to make a decision, "Do I stay, or do I go?" This was some months prior to our meeting with George:

George: (To Helen) Are you of Irish heritage?

Helen: Slight.

George: It's interesting, I see St. Patrick over your head but I don't see you in this context.

Ron: She's showing her name.

George: All right, all right, don't say anything. Yeah, but it's not—you see I saw St. Patrick appear before and that's what made me give out Patty but now I don't see it.

We later realized that the name he had not been able to determine earlier was Erin's friend, Erinn Nabong. She and I have become very close friends and she was a member of ASP, as was our Erin:

George: Me, of all people, I'm of that heritage, I should know what the hell she's talking about. All right, without telling me, don't say anything, she obviously has a very stereotypical Irish name, or obviously Irish sounding.

Ron and Helen: Irish sounding, yes.

George: Oh. Let's see, maybe I'll think of my Irish cousins, maybe one of them has the same name and she'll say that's it. No, it's a Gaelic word. [This I did not know.] (Looking upward) Ummm—I don't speak Gaelic, Hon. So don't say it anyway. Yes, she tells me I know what it is. I've probably heard it a hundred times in my lifetime. Oh, wait a minute, that's right, the flag says "Erin Go Bragh," which is "Long Live Ireland," so it's got to be Erin, I guess.

Ron and Helen: Yes.

George: I've never heard of anyone having the name "Go Bragh."

When we returned home from New York, I called Erinn Nabong to see if Erin had ever mentioned what was on the Irish flag. She laughed and said, yes, that on St. Patrick's day Erin would march around the pub with a glass of green beer shouting "Erin Go Bragh, Erin Forever":

George: Was she also called by a nickname of some sort?

Ron and Helen: Yes.

George: Like she says, like "Errie" or something?

Ron and Helen: No.

George: She said something else, the actual name is Erin,

obviously, but she's known by something else.

Ron and Helen: Yes.

George: She does give me the feeling there's a nickname as well.

Erin had been called "Fish" by all her friends for years and years so we did not understand why George couldn't perceive this. We were going for the obvious. Four days later, while walking to the gate at Kennedy Airport, I remembered my pet name for her, one I used only when the two of us were together, Errnie (air-nee). Even Ron was not aware of this name although Lizz said she had heard me use it at some time in the past. This was a special something only between Erin and me:

George: Her sister dreamed about her?

Helen: Yes.

George: Yes, she says she's come to Lizz in dreams and tell her, "You've heard from Erin twice. Not only in dreams but also through this manner of discerning." You know she's all right, she just doubly reassures it. A very friendly person?

Ron: Yes.

George: You know, apparently made friends and had a job in ten minutes.

Ron: Yes.

George: Again she says, "I'm not shocked by death. I know I'm going to pass on," and she also was ready to adjust to the next stage of the passing. It's funny, was she a little afraid at the end? Might of kept it to herself, a little spooked, but she says, "It's like walking from this room to the next. There's nothing to fear but fear itself."

Is she very fond of children?

Ron: Yes.

George: She says she works with children in the next stage, especially children who come over frightened. She has a very—even though she's a young woman, she has a very motherly way about her. Well, unquestionably, even though I warned people at the beginning that you might not hear from whom you would like to, in her case that doesn't hold.

Ron: That's right.

George: You would definitely have heard from her one way or another. She said she would have found a way to get through. Yeah, again, she didn't have a brother did she or somebody very close to her, like a brother?

Ron: Yes.

Helen: There was a close friend.

George: Yeah, a male though

Helen: A very close friend.

George: Yeah, because she's talking about somebody that's close to her like a brother. So if you have contact with him, tell him you've heard from Erin. And she calls out, as well. It's funny, even though she had this problem it's like it still doesn't get her down. She moves on courageously into the next stage of life and certainly makes her mark on this world before she leaves. And she's very thankful for all the people who came to the wake and funeral because, as she says, she doesn't want to sound conceited but she knew she was liked but it was tremendous support for you, her parents and family. That's why she's pleased with the people who took the time to show that support. Very appreciative person.

George: (To Ron) She wishes you a "Happy Father's Day" a little early but she knows you can't be here in June so she sends the red roses to you as in greeting.

Ron always puts a red rose by Erin's picture in his office on special occasions such as her birthday, etc., so this made sense to us:

George: (To Ron) Is there a John passed on, too? It seems to be your side of the family. He seems to be around your father.

Ron: Not that I can recall.

George: I'll have to leave it with you. Maybe somebody you can't think of right now.

Ron's father had a brother named Jake. He was one of seventeen children and there is very little history on any of them. It is possible, I suppose, that John and Jake would come through to George in a similar way, but that is just a guess on my part:

George: Also, a Daniel, passed on, or living? Your daughter mentioned him, but again I'm sure she had a million friends.

Helen: She had a lot we didn't know.

George: I'm going to leave it with you.

Helen: I don't know right now.

We later remembered a Daniel from high school days:

George: I think with this they're going to step aside. They seem to be fading down. Your father (to Ron), did he actually like abandon you emotionally?

Ron: Yes.

George: 'Cause, again, he keeps apologizing for that. You don't hold it against him, he knows that, but he wants to make that declaration all the same. I think with that they're going to close because both your parents go back and like the different grandparents around you are doing the same. But your father's glad of having the opportunity to come in to finally clean the slate, him and your mother. Your father inclined to drink?

Ron: Yes.

George: Yes, he apologizes for a drinking problem and certainly your mother kind of got caught in the middle of everything but things were very difficult, but certainly you've risen above these obstacles in your life and have achieved. As your father says, in that case he's very happy that you have achieved and you put him to shame in the sense that you overcame. But they go back, certainly asking that you remember to pray for them, and your daughter's going back and she sends her love to the two of you, deeply, and her sister. She says, "Until we all meet again." So she says in the meantime, certainly remember her with love as you do from your stage as she does from her stage, "Until we meet again." And with that she signs off, and the others do, too.

Our taping was of very poor quality, slowed and stopped in places, and as a result several things which we remember being said did not record. They are as follows:

George: She says she has sent you many signs?

Helen: Yes, she has.

George: You're here to verify what you already know.

There was also, I believe, something mentioned about the honor at school that did not record, and about presenting me with white roses.

• • • •

Following our meeting with George, Ron and I spent several days sightseeing in New York City. On two different occasions we both felt Erin's presence. The first was when we walked into Battery Park and saw the Statue of Liberty in the harbor. My immediate reaction was a terrible sinking feeling, Erin would never get to see this, but then I had the strangest sensation and turned and looked at Ron and said, "She is right here, in-between us." It was a really overwhelming feeling of her standing there with us. His reply was, "I know she is."

The second time on this trip when we both were aware of her presence was while we were walking through Greenwich Village. This was an area Erin would have dearly loved. The sensation was very strong for both of us.

• • • •

One evening several months after we returned from New York as we were driving home from a dinner, I could sense her in the back seat, in the center of the seat with arms both stretched out high on the seat back. This feeling was so intense that I even turned to look. The same feeling you might have when you know someone is coming close to you but your back is turned and you neither see nor hear them, but you know someone is there. You sense it in your back.

I am now experiencing her presence much more often and it is usually, but not always, in the limbo stage where a person is not quite awake but still not asleep. Just for a split second, she is there. Several times it has happened while I am completely awake, as I have sat down at the computer to work on this manuscript and, just for an instant, she is there. It is similar to seeing someone within your peripheral vision.

• • • •

Several months after our trip to Long Island, I told a friend to go to the same library where I had found *We Don't Die* because she had expressed an interest in reading it. She later related to me that it was not there, not on the shelves or in the computer. I went back to check and she was correct; there was no longer a trace of this book in the library where I had found it the preceding summer.

Chapter Eleven

*I*n March, 1992, I was introduced to a wonderful woman I shall refer to as Bea in this writing in order to protect her privacy. She, like George Anderson, has been given the gift of psychic ability. Our first meeting was to be on a casual basis. I had gone with several friends, one of whom was to have a reading, and I remember standing off to one side and being somewhat nervous as Bea greeted the others. She came to me and took my hands in hers and said, "And this must be Helen," and gave me one of the warmest, most enveloping hugs I have ever experienced. Bea later mentioned she would also like to meet privately with me that day.

Later that afternoon the two of us talked and she told me the reason she had needed to speak to me was that when she had hugged me a sweet little voice told her, "Talk to her today, she has waited long enough." I had been attempting to meet Bea for nearly eight months but had been so caught up in selling our house, making a move, etc., that the opportunity to do so just had not materialized.

I do not have a tape of this first meeting, as I do of the others, as this was just a short visit. We talked of many things in a short time but one stands out above all others. She told me she was seeing two circles, one small and one larger, a gold bracelet and a gold ring. She then saw a single, very shiny stone in the ring. I knew immediately what this meant. The back of my engagement ring had worn through and had resided in my jewel case for several years and I had planned on having a gold ankle bracelet of Erin's melted down to become part of the ring when I had it repaired. Several months prior to my meeting with Bea, I had attempted to do this but, much to my dismay, was unable to do so as I was told the solder in the bracelet would weaken the ring. I had the single diamond polished and reset in a new band in the usual way.

Six weeks later I again met with Bea and have chosen portions of the taped reading to be used here:

Bea: I'm hearing someone calling you "Moms." Did Erin call you "Moms?"

Helen: Sometimes, I think. I know Mom all the time.

Bea: Yes, but this is "Moms," you know the "gentle Moms." Like, "Oh, Moms."

Helen: She did, takes a while sometimes.

Bea: That's all right. I can understand that because my daughters would call me something occasionally a little different from what they would ordinarily and that was always at one of those nice gentle times, but this is "Moms."

Well, how do I want to put this. She knew that there would be a very close confirmation because—or communication with you and your husband, the two of you. It's as though she brings the two of you together. She knew there would be a very close communication with you because that was one of the—hard to say this— because it was almost as though it was a stipulation that she made when she turned and realized that she had left this earth plane. It was that she would go knowing that was what she was supposed to do. In other words, that she was fulfilling a commitment of her own but the circumstances were that she would go at that time, at the time when she was called, with the stipulation that she would be able to communicate with the two of you and, of course, she has held to that already. And she has a great deal to learn also about the communication that goes on between the spiritual realm and the human realm, but right now it seems unusual, it seems magical, but it is not at all. It is not at all. It is due to the fact that the human on this earth plane has had so many disappointments, has had so many non-truths given to him that the faith is not as strong as it should be. That there is nothing that is more real than the communication, and what those in the spirit world must do is to work not to bring the communication, they have that, but it is to try to learn the ways all over again of the human in trying to communicate with them. Often times there is real difficulty with one human communicating with another human. And that will come. That is a commitment she made when she left this earth plane and it was accepted and so will it be.

Did she have a little brown mole on her leg?

Helen: Not that I remember.

Bea: This was one that she had as a baby, almost like I'm hearing "beauty mark." Maybe that was something that she had questioned and you said that's a beauty mark, but I'm seeing this leg with a mole on it.

Helen: I don't know, that just doesn't ring a bell at all.

Bea: That's all right. That's just one of those little minor things but when they come in they oftentimes make you jog your memory for it. I feel as though she is showing it. It's like, "Oh, Mom."

Helen: I can just hear her say that (laughter). She knows I've never been good at charades.

I later recalled having many discussions with Erin about the moles she had on various areas of her body. I remember telling her to just think of them as beauty marks:

Bea: Oh, she's so dear, she's so dear. Things have started she feels, things have begun. There have been some mystical things which have happened since she's gone and you've listened to them. And you've responded to them and she is very positive, very positive, that all this is going to be. She has no doubts. She knows she's going to make a difference. She's going to be a very wonderful guide but also I think she's going to be one of those who will help a great many others who make their transition—the same feeling as though she's going to be a very wonderful spiritual guide for many people. But mainly between families and children, offspring, offspring. When you feel blue about it, think of something that is beautiful that you will be doing with her from now on, instead of, I wish I could have this now. You do, it's already happened. So you use the thought of the love you had for her at that time to bring into communication. All you do at that time is say to her, I remember when we did such and such and so and so and it's just as beautiful now as it was then—you know that sort of thing so, and, of course, that bond becomes so strong because you have already been bonded, the two of you during your lifetime, but this is the time now for the very, very strong bonding of the spiritual, in the spiritual level.

• • • •

Bea: Think of Erin as one of the biggest blessings you could possibly have because think of the people who don't have that blessing in their life, they are empty.

• • • •

Bea: I don't know what the answer to this is and I have asked, but it seems important. It seems important and I don't understand why, so if I can't find that answer I'm not supposed to have it but for some reason I'm supposed to follow it. To tell you that, this seems very unusual, but it's important for you to have fresh lavender in your home.

Helen: Fresh lavender?

Bea: Uh huh. The lavender plant, you know.

Helen: The color makes sense.

Bea: Does it?

Helen: Yes.

Bea: O.K.

Helen: Yes, not as a plant but as a color.

Bea: Oh. Oh, all right, because it's the lavender. O.K.

Helen: Yes. (laughter)

Bea: No wonder I couldn't get an answer.

Helen: (laughing) Oh, yes.

Bea: O.K., but why are they supposed to have a lavender plant? Takes awhile for me to get these things, too. I mean I always ask for—.

Helen: I hoped the color would be mentioned. (laughter) It's very significant. Do you want me to tell you what it means?

Bea: Yes, I would love to know if you don't mind sharing it.

Helen: When she was in high school, in junior high and in high school, in fact for years, she wore every shade of purple. We dyed all the white clothes in the house, we dyed them purple. It was her trademark. So I was hoping some shade of purple or lavender would be mentioned. But yes, very significant. Purple bras, purple tennis shoes.

Bea: Isn't that funny because all I could think of was the importance there and I thought it was the lavender plant.

Helen: That makes me feel so good.

Bea: Oh, yes. Even though you've got sort of a stupid medium here—well all I could see was the lavender flower, you see, you know. Oh, yes. Well it smells pretty good, too, that lavender scent. A giggle or two.

Helen: A giggle or two, oh, yes.

Bea: Yes, this is a giggle, not a laugh outward, she's giggling.

• • • •

Bea: I'm hearing a song and perhaps this is one that Erin enjoyed a great deal and I'm hearing it as something that was sung over and over and over again. The group she was with, they sang it over and over and there was a guitar accompaniment, I don't know whether it was a mandolin or another string instrument, and they used to get together and they'd laugh and sing with it but it has a very, very deep meaning to it and I don't know what it was. It was something to do with, you are my hero, you are my hero and the wind beneath the eagle's wings.

Helen: Yes!

Bea: Really.

Helen: Yes, my husband gave it to me, the tape, on my first birthday after we lost Erin. It was the way he had of telling me how he felt about me, that I was his hero, the wind beneath his wings. Oh Bea, she knows everything that goes on. She's with us.

Bea: Oh, my.

Helen: It was his gift to me. We were stopped for construction on the highway and we played it and we both cried because we weren't communicating.

Bea: And there is a song?

Helen: Yes, it's called "Wind Beneath My Wings." It's, "Have

I ever told you you're my hero and you're all I ever want to be." Oh Bea, what a gift.

I had played this tape over and over and still do:

Bea: Oh my goodness.

Helen: She just keeps giving the gifts.

Bea: I'm going to have to cut this off. I've got tears rolling down my face and my nose is running. I'm going to have to cut this off, we're both crying.

At this visit, prior to taping, Bea also mentioned that Erin was very artistic. One example she used was that Erin had a real knack of putting clothes together. This was very true; Erin's artistic quality was also mentioned by George:

• • • •

Bea: I'm just being thanked, too, for being able to tell you what they wanted to tell you.

• • • •

Bea: We ask that whatever has come through will be for the highest good of this dear one who sits here with me and for those, particularly this one who has gone beyond, just beyond, with only a thin veil between and that is penetrable when there is love.

• • • •

Bea: This is July 8, 1992, and we're having a little joint reading here again for Helen from Bea and something to add to our records together. A lavender light comes in here so you know what that means.

Helen: That's right.

Bea: Absolutely beautiful lavender light. Very brilliant lavender. Not a deep purple, a lavender, and it's very spiky because it's the energy that's so powerful going out in spikes all around from the center of this lavender light and going out into the spikes of pure white light that goes from those lavender spikes. So very, very much a center here of energy and of certainly that dear one who gladly comes in here again. Lots of thank yous and beauty.

Hmmm. Well we know who's bringing this in and we know very well what you're going to have to go out and get and that is a very, pale violet plant, pale blue, and it has this little white edging of white around each of the petals. It's a full, it seems to be a very full blossom that is on it but it is edged with white. It's edged with white and there will be one which you will see, which you will look for, of course, but you'll be guided to. But it must come in, it must come in for you. It will be a large violet eventually because there is such great love with it that not even artificial feeding will be needed. But it's there and that's—so many gifts—but that is very necessary for you to have so you can see it for yourself. It seems there would be a potted violet for you every day if it were possible. She is there always. Each time she enters the house she brings in a flower or a plant or a bouquet. Even though it is unseen it is always there and there will be times you will smell the floral scent even though you cannot see the bouquet. She's very close.

Soon after this meeting with Bea I found my violet. It seemed nearly every store I entered had white edged violets for sale but since that time I very rarely see them. Regular violets, yes, but not the ones with the little "blanket stitch" edging. It now measures 15-16" across. This is amazing growth because the plant was very small when I purchased it, the size you get for $2.99:

Bea: A great deal of enthusiasm. "Oh, Mom, it's beautiful." She is very happy. "It's beautiful." She wants to assure you how beautiful things are, how beautiful she feels and how beautiful that life is that she is experiencing right now, life after life. "Unbelievable in its beauty, but it is very necessary to also know that it's very beautiful when you can see the beauty. It is not there unless the heart can see the beauty." Her word for you this day.
  Is your cat white?

Helen: No.

Bea: Well there's a white cat in here. Almost as though maybe that's what she wants you—. Maybe it's coming around, but I don't get that it's coming directly from her but having her influence here and her vibration so close. This fluffy little white cat, it looks like a kitten.

Helen: We've been wanting to get Lizz a cat.

Bea: There it is.

Helen: We thought she needed something.

Bea: There it is and it's a little furry...long furred white kitten. Not very old, not very old.

Helen: That's it then.

Bea: Uh hum. Gotta be white, all white. And that will come, too. You'll know exactly where that is. Well, you'll know exactly how that one is going to come to you. Ah, it's fun. There's a little bit of leaping around and clapping of hands here. She's just, she's so exuberant. She's so exuberant, she's so happy about things, and the acceptance is so great. Because this is what she wants, that is why she is so exuberant. Because the acceptance is there and she knows it. She is—that she is getting through to you and it's wonderful. She's sharing with you just as you're sharing your love with her.

The cat never made it into our lives. Perhaps the mention of the cat was just to let us know that Erin is aware of our daily activities. In other words, that she knew we were looking for a cat for Lizz at that time. Or it could be that she was letting us know that she had something to do with a four month old kitten appearing on our doorstep November 1, 1990. When I picked up the kitten that night, she reached up and patted me on the face. It was almost as though she was telling me, "It's O.K., it's O.K. And with that little pat I felt something I thought I wouuld never feel again. I felt joy.

For the first several weeks after she adopted us, it was almost as though she didn't want to play favorites with Ron and me. In the evenings she would alternate between sitting on Ron and then back to me—ten minutes on his lap and then back over onto mine. She would sometimes sit behind me on the back of the couch and reach around and give my face a pat. After several weeks of this, her behavior became more normal for a cat.

Most of what is related by Bea seems to be clues for the recipient of the reading to understand. Bea's interpretation is often very broad. A good example is the song she heard

Erin and a group singing. I knew immediately what was meant but it did not come through to Bea as my listening to a tape or that it had been given to me by Ron:

Bea: She has a lot of work to do. She has a lot of work to do and she's going into that higher learning and it is beautiful because she's actually going into it a little bit earlier than was expected and it is a beginning of truth right now. A good many things which she thought of as truth have been pushed aside to receive the real truth, which she wanted and which she is accepting, and what she not only has learned as truth but which is guiding her towards that place of wisdom which she will achieve one day.

  First and foremost, she is a beautiful young teacher and this is what she's studying for, and I'm seeing that this is the task she will take on for others on this earth that need very much the teaching and the touching of the inner self. Many things will be brought to others when she has completed the path she's on now. It's a beautiful path. There is such love. There is such exuberance. There is such happiness and there is such understanding. She is just so wide open to everything that is necessary. She's learning that many things that she thought she knew were only expanded in the right way, in the way of truth. Many areas that she felt she should cling to because they were truth have been changed for her just a bit so that the wisdom—it was if the wisdom and the result of what she believed in became the wisdom, and so therefore there were many changes. However subtle, there were changes and she has accepted them fully and completely and that's why she is on the path of the teacher for others. This is the task, this is the work that she will do.

• • • •

Bea: Did she ever wonder or ask you why you didn't wear yellow? Because you look good in yellow, and you don't think you look good in yellow.

Helen: I have a yellow blouse that I always feel good when I wear it. It was a blouse I had when she was with us.

Bea: Well, did she ever voice that you didn't wear enough yellow?

Helen: No, not that I recall.

Bea: Because she's seeing you, and this is brought out as if you should wear the yellow of the sun and that was a good expression for you. It's a particular color that will be very good for you. (Laughter) She's going to make you go out and buy some clothes. There's a yellow suit, I see you in a yellow suit, a two-piece yellow suit. A very nicely, femininely tailored suit, two pieces and it's something you wouldn't look at twice if you hadn't heard about this but it's going to be right there and you're going to remember it and I can see the blouse that's under it. It's like a silk—oh, what do I want to say. Silk. Oh, what are they called, the little shell, you know, and there is some color with it. Some color in it, whether it's stripes or what it is, I just see, I see different colors. But very lovely, very pretty, which will accentuate this yellow suit and will give you a lot of joy and happiness in wearing it. Hmmm (laughter), it's like she drew a great deep breath. Well, she'll be shopping with you, too.

When we were in Sitka, Alaska the previous month, while

browsing through various shops I had found a suit identical to the one Bea had described. It was my size and I was tempted to try it on but talked myself out of it by convincing myself I don't really look good in yellow and that I probably wouldn't wear a tailored suit very often as I dress very casually. I think I was chastised, through Bea, for not buying that suit:

· · · ·

Bea: My goodness, she's close to you. Ah. Did she have a way of when she walked, if your husband was sitting in a chair or something, did she have a way of walking by his chair and leaning out as she passed him and patting him a couple times on the top of the head?

Helen: Probably. That is something he would remember.

Bea: Just a little pat pat.

Helen: Probably.

Bea: Just a little pat pat as she went by.

Helen: She was very affectionate.

Bea: You can ask him about that because it's as though when she goes by anytime there's just a little pat pat.

I realized later that a little pat pat is what I always do when I'm passing by Ron. Several days after meeting with Bea I caught myself giving Ron a pat as I was walking by where he was sitting. It is such an unconscious habit of so many years I had not made the connection.

· · · ·

Bea: It's a beautiful garden I'm seeing. Just an absolutely beautiful garden. There is a fountain in the middle and it's cherubs and angels and what not on this lovely base of this fountain that flows up like an umbrella type, or thing, of water. But all around the edge of it, all around the edge of this little pond, pool, nothing but lavender tulips, lavender tulips....There's a lot of playing around among those tulips. They're tall and they're beautiful, big, and it's a very expansive garden. A very beautiful garden and if you look around it's endless with special blooms and special areas for special flowers, but all around the edge of this lovely little pool are these tall beautiful lavender tulips.

Helen: I wonder if she's telling us she was at Buchart Gardens with us. [I remembered later overhearing someone saying how beautiful the tulips were in the Spring.]

Bea: Oh, well, it could well be. Was there a fountain there?

Helen: There were several.

Bea: I've been in Buchart Gardens, too, but unfortunately those were the war years when they were not maintained.

Helen: They were beautiful.

Bea: Of course, that's the lavender color I saw and the white radiating out from the spikes of the energies....Boy, I'm getting all weepy here. It's just too special.

Bea: Oh, she brings so much love in here and in so many different ways and I'm sure you must feel her. The energy is just all around, just all around. Beautiful soul she is. How special to have her here on this earth plane for that length of time even. Indeed were you blessed. She knew what she was doing. Every soul chooses the parents.

. . . .

Bea: She's been milling around here so close. She's very patient with me when I can't describe things as I should or things that there aren't words for.

At this point we neglected to turn over the tape so some of this has to be from memory. Bea proceeded to describe a garden and a young women in a beautiful white dress. As she spoke she used her hands to show how the dress was designed, the neckline in particular. It was close to an exact description of the dress Erin's friend, Lori, had chosen for her wedding the previous month. Lori's wedding took place in a lovely, large back yard:

Helen: It was a very, very close friend and very difficult for Ron and I to go to.

Bea: Yes.

Helen: But we did.

Bea: Oh, very definitely. But this was a very old fashioned, beautiful sensitive feeling of purity with this girl. Just lovely.

Helen: I kind of expected some words of a song to come in because they played a song that had some meaning for us from a time past.

Bea: It didn't, no, just her going into the garden and the feeling that there was with it. The beauty of the garden, the beauty of her actually. She had a very pure soul but I didn't hear the music. I could see the garden expanding out. Not that it was a real—that the garden expanded that far out, it was how she felt about this garden that was so expansive. Very, very pure expanding thoughts there. With a true meaning of what she wanted as far as marriage was concerned.

• • • •

Bea: The Rose, was that the name of the music?

Helen: The what?

Bea: The Rose?

Helen: No.

Bea: No. A big beautiful huge, red rose and I could hear the music with it.

Helen: You did. There was a significant happening in the last month with a rose.

Bea: Beautiful, just beautiful. And the music was just beautiful. Whatever it was for a confirmation, I think you got it.

In June, on the third anniversary of Erin's transition, while we were on a cruise in Alaska, we had slipped up on deck to a private spot and dropped roses into the water to commemorate the day. And, as previously mentioned, Ron always puts a red rose near her picture on the desk in his office for every special occasion, so, as with our meeting with George Anderson when symbolic red roses were presented to Ron, this had a very significant meaning to us.

Chapter
Twelve

$\mathscr{I}$n our session with George Anderson it was mentioned that Erin had come in dreams; the following are dreams experienced by some of Erin's friends and family:

One evening during the summer of 1991, I had fallen asleep while sitting on the couch and I dreamed that Erin was standing directly in front of me. I remember being very startled and saying, "Why, it's Erin," and waking up with a jolt; she seemed so very real. I discounted this as a normal dream until I later talked to one of Erin's friends and told her of this experience. She was rather taken aback because she had exactly the same dream during this same time period.

Wendy Cole Clark related the following dream to me:

Wendy dreamed that she was sleeping between her parents in a big bed. In this dream, she awoke to find Erin standing at the foot of the bed. Erin appeared completely white, not transparent or ghostly, merely everything about Erin was white in color, her clothes, her hair, and her skin. Wendy sat up and moved to the edge of the bed where Erin instructed her to "keep writing." "But what do I write about?" asked Wendy. "You can write about anything," Erin answered. When Wendy pressed her for an example, Erin said she could write about pregnancy and childbirth. "What it's like to have a baby." Wendy's feeling was that Erin meant the emotional aspect rather than the physical. Then to further her explanation, Erin showed Wendy a couple of coffee table books and told her that she could look at them for ideas.

Overcome with emotion, Wendy then reached out to touch Erin but when she touched Erin's sleeve, Erin disappeared. Wendy, still dreaming, was very startled and felt the need to tell her mother that Erin had visited her, so she woke up her mother and said, "Mom! Erin was here! Erin was here!" Her mother was very comforting but Wendy sensed that she did not believe Erin had actually appeared. At this point, Wendy turned away from her mother and noticed the two coffee table books on the nightstand. She turned to her mother and explained that Erin had left those books there. Wendy's mother had no other choice but to believe her because the books had not been beside the bed before they had gone to sleep, in fact, the books had never before been in their home.

After Wendy and her mother talked about what had happened, Wendy climbed back into bed between her parents. After her parents had gone back to sleep, Erin came back and stood at the foot of the bed. She was still entirely white. Wendy felt that Erin was there to reassure her that her visit was real. She wanted to touch Erin again but knew that if she did Erin might disappear. Wanting Erin to stay with her forever, Wendy sat quietly and concentrated on the white form of her friend. Erin told her to "keep writing" once again. She disappeared on her own accord. Thus the dream ended.

It was amazing how easily Wendy related this dream to me because it had been over four years since it had happened. When I mentioned this to her, she concurred, saying she has never recalled her dreams so vividly, especially after such an extended period of time. It was different than any dream she could remember ever having.

In another dream experienced by a friend, Erin appeared surrounded by a shining light and dressed in a long white gown. Her hair was longer, more, as described to me, as it had been as a small child. She said she had been given a very important job to do but that she wasn't allowed to tell what it was. Erin appeared quite overwhelmed that she had been assigned such an important task and was uncertain of her worthiness. This dream ended with Erin saying, "I have to go now. I'm dead, you know."

In another instance, Erin came to this same person in a dream and related that Lucy (Lucille Ball) was there but that she hadn't seen her. They had both shared a love for the "I Love Lucy" shows.

Another friend of Erin's, whom I will call Joy, recounted the following dream to me:

Joy and some of her friends had been out celebrating on the eve of their graduation from college. Soon after falling asleep that night, Joy said it was almost as though she had awakened to find Erin sitting on the bed. "I can't believe you're here," she told Erin. "Well, I just wanted to tell you congratulations," Erin replied.

Joy related to me that not much was actually spoken but that images of all the good times they had had together flashed through her mind. She looked at Erin and Erin laughed; Joy knew that Erin was experiencing the same images she was. They were communicating in a telepathic manner.

Erin then said, "Have a really good time. I wish I could be there."

The following dream was contributed by Erin's cousin, Blake Clark:

"Erin has come to me in dreams on several occasions....

Recently in a dream I was talking with Erin in the wings of a small school's stage. I have always admired Erin and am in awe of the choices she made during her time here on

Earth. I have often thought that she accomplished more in twenty years than most people do in a lifetime. So this time when I 'ran into' Erin I was curious. I asked her if she had done everything she wanted to do while she was here. Her answer was a laughing, 'Of course not.' I rephrased the question. 'Did you do everything you were SUPPOSED to do when you were here?' Her answer was very reassuring and all Erin. 'Well, Blake, it's not like they give you a pop quiz or anything when you pass over.' And smiling as she said that, our conversation came to an end."

A young woman I will refer to as Gerri had a dream about Erin in October, 1989, in which Erin invited Gerri to accompany her to a movie. After the movie started, Gerri turned and looked at Erin and asked her, "Why did you bring me to such an old movie?" Erin's laughing reply was, "Shut up, and watch the movie." The movie was *Earthquake*. The Loma Prieta Earthquake occurred in the San Francisco Bay Area, where we were living at the time, the following day.

I had the following dream. I was in a car and Erin was with me. I was going to the optometrist to have my eyes checked and as we drove along I realized that I wasn't wearing my glasses. I said, "This really isn't my day." I was upset because this meant I would have to be completely retested since I didn't have the old lenses with me. Erin didn't say anything during all of this.

We then came to a roadblock where construction was

being done. I drove up close to the barricade and then realized there were two holes in the pavement and I drove over them. I somehow thought it was safe because the barricade was on the other side of this area. The front tire went into one of these holes and the car tipped to one side. There was a man in a business suit who was directing a crane operator to put a giant hook on the car and pull us out of the hole. Everyone was moving very slowly. Suddenly the hole became larger and the car started to slip down beneath the street. I didn't feel any panic and Erin was very calm. We just kept floating downward, and at one point I rolled up the window so we wouldn't fall out. I looked out the window and said, "It must really be a long way down there." I told Erin that we would probably crash when we got to the bottom and to be prepared. I think I just assumed we would die when we hit bottom, wherever that was, but there was no feeling of fear.

I then realized that Erin had been sitting there drawing while we went down into the semi-darkness. It was as though we could see a wall as we passed, there was enough light for that. The feeling was of complete calm and peace with a sensation of floating. It was definitely not a usual dream of falling where you wake up in a state of panic. Erin then handed me her drawings. There was a series of pictures but I can recall only one. It was the outline of a person, similar to a chalk drawing made by the police at a crime scene. What I do remember vividly is the writing that accompanied the first picture. It read, "Erin Going." I then started to wake up and was almost overcome with guilt feelings. I had driven over those holes even though something seemed to tell me that I shouldn't; that feeling was simultaneous with the act of actually driving up to the barricade. Then the thought came into my mind, "But you couldn't see, you didn't have your glasses on," and I felt absolute relief.

As I awakened I had the very strong feeling that what I had experienced was Erin letting me know how she felt as she went through the tunnel. (Bea has indicated she thinks perhaps it was more the feelings Erin experienced when leaving her body.) Also, since Erin's death I have struggled with intense feelings of guilt, thinking that if I had only been more perceptive perhaps her death could have been prevented. I believe this dream was to help me understand that there was no way for me to have foreseen the final outcome of her illness as I could not "see" what was ahead.

The following incident happened in the past year. I was reading before retiring and had almost fallen asleep with the book still open in my hands. I was in that twilight area where you aren't completely asleep but not awake either. I was starting to dream when I felt Erin's cheek against my lips. She had allowed me to kiss her; the skin on her face had exactly the same softness and texture as it always had. The interesting thing was that the kiss was not connected in any way with the dream I was having. It was more like an overlay or a simultaneous happening.

SYNCHRONICITY: Coincidence of events that seem to be

meaningfully related.

Late in July, 1992, Bea called one morning and asked if this was a special day for me. I said, no, that it was just a normal day. She persisted, "Are you sure?" She then told me that during meditation that morning she had been asked by Erin to let me know I was being sent a Sterling Silver Rose, a lavender rose. I had no idea why as it was just an ordinary day, but as soon as I hung up the phone, I realized the significance. The day before I had spent a large amount of time on the phone calling various government representatives to protest the dumping of very usable fruit in the Central Valley area. Erin had always chided me for "talking a good story" but never following through on issues about which I have very strong feelings. It was several days after this call from Bea that we noticed the Sterling Silver Rose in the parking lot at the winery, which I have written about in an earlier chapter.

When the following event transpired I did not realize what an amazing coincidence it really was because we were so involved in the serious turn Erin's illness had taken. It was the evening of the day Erin was diagnosed with pneumocystis pneumonia. We had gone home from the hospital to take care of the dog and get a little sleep and I sat down for a few minutes to look at the newspaper and in the paper there was a very large article about pneumocystis pneumonia and how very serious it is. Up until that point, I had never read anything about this type of pneumonia.

Another meaningful synchronicity happened one day as I was driving home following a visit to Bea. A short distance from her house a car exiting from a shopping center pulled in front of mine, the license plate read "E R I N N."

We experienced a similar coincidence the summer before when we were waiting to embark on an Alaskan cruise. We had time to do some sightseeing in Seattle before we boarded our ship so we were having a good time going through the various shops. We were browsing through a bookstore when I had a strong feeling that I should turn around. The shelf behind me was full of books on fish and tacked to the shelf was a small slip of white paper with the word "FISH," followed by a drawing of a fish with little bubbles coming out of its mouth, an exact duplicate of how Erin signed her nickname.

A short time later we walked into a gift shop and I immediately saw a rack of miniature license plates that have names on them; there was a full row of them with the name Erin. Many more than you would expect to find of one particular name.

On the final morning of our cruise, as our ship was proceeding to dock in Juneau, Alaska, the captain was playing a tape that was broadcast throughout the ship and I was very startled to hear words that spoke of smiling even when your heart is breaking. It seemed almost too appropriate to be a coincidence, and it was rather a strange choice of music for entering port after a week at sea. As I have mentioned earlier, the anniversary of Erin's death was during the week we were on the cruise.

My sister Linda also had a very interesting incident take place starting in December, 1992. During a very severe ice storm she had braved the elements in an attempt to find a butterfly necklace because she had suddenly had a very strong feeling it was important that she do so. However, Linda was unable to find one that day.

Approximately six weeks later as Linda was gathering old newspapers to take to the recycler, a stack of papers fell over and she noticed an ad for jewelry. Prominently displayed in this ad was a butterfly necklace. The date on the newspaper was in the same time frame as when Linda had first felt the need to buy this particular necklace. She immediately went to this store, the necklace was still there, and Linda purchased it. The store also happened to be the same department store chain that employs Erin's father and was the store he worked in at the time of Erin's birth.

Several days after Erin's death, a friend of both Lizz and Erin contacted Lizz to ask her what time Erin's death had occurred. She was quite shaken when told it was 4:15 a.m. because her clock had stopped at that exact time the morning of Erin's passing.

While sitting on the couch watching TV one evening during

the summer of 1989, I had a strong sensation of Erin's presence beside me. When she was ill her legs ached from the chemotherapy treatment and she would like to have Ron or me rub them. The feeling I had was of Erin's legs stretched out to be rubbed. It was such a strong sensation that I reached out to touch her leg. And I did feel it, even the slight stubble of hair growing back. I thought it was because I so desperately wanted her presence to be there but several weeks later Ron told me something that made me realize it was much more than that. He had experienced the exact same sensations even down to the feeling of the stubble on her legs at approximately this same time. I had not mentioned my experience to him prior to this.

Dr. Love told me that she had never given much thought to reincarnation but that for some reason on the Saturday night when it had become obvious that Erin was losing her fight to live, she and her husband had stayed up all night talking about the possibility of reincarnation. This seemed to be somewhat of a puzzle to her because she was not raised to believe in this possibility and, as I mentioned before, had never given the concept much thought.

Several years ago I happened to read a gardening article about a buddleia bush, also known as a butterfly bush because it tends to attract butterflies, and we had tried to find one at various nurseries, all to no avail. We had several bare spots in our yard due to the loss of shrubs from a hard freeze and we really wanted to find a buddleia bush to fill in these areas. We finally gave up and decided to put in something else. I was on my way to a garden shop to pick up several trees so we could plant them the next day when I drove by a nursery and noticed a sign indicating a sale on trees. I decided to stop and check prices, hoping I could get a better buy on the trees we had finally chosen to plant. I went in and looked around but they didn't have the variety I wanted. I started to leave when a sign caught my eye—BUDDLEIA, BUTTERFLY BUSH. They had a special shipment of them and at a very good price. For some reason I had imagined them with a bright pink or orange flower, the article I had read had not mentioned the color, but they were covered with tiny lavender blossoms. I bought three. I thought it was quite amazing that after looking for this bush for at least two years, I finally found it after I had completely given up and was on my way to buy something else. It could not have been more perfect timing.

Ron had a strange occurrence at the store where he works. He began to notice that shipments that were coming in would have a good assortment of colors with the exception of one; there would often be just one purple garment. Or he would walk by a rack of clothes and notice again that there was only one in the color purple. This happened so often that others in the store started to bring it to his attention. This interesting phenomenon continued to happen most of that winter.

Last fall our synchronicities took an amusing turn. It does-n't directly relate to this book but it does point out perhaps how often so-called coincidences happen and we really don't notice them.

My niece was visiting us, and Ron and she and I were getting ready to retire for the evening, putting the dog out for a few minutes and getting her bed out, etc. I did some-thing really dumb (I don't even remember what it was now) and Ron put his arm around me and said, "Say goodnight, Gracie." (From the days of the George Burns and Gracie Allen TV show.) I, of course, said, "Goodnight, Gracie" and by the next morning we had all forgotten the incident.

The next day we decided to go to an art festival that we usually try to attend each year. This was Labor Day Weekend so many stores had merchandise displayed in front of their buildings to catch the eye of motorists. As we passed one shop, I did a complete double take; there were throw pillows piled in front of the shop and one had writing on it that read, "Say goodnight, Gracie." I think perhaps this goes to prove that not all coincidences have to be of a seri-ous nature. It certainly gave the three of us a good laugh.

Chapter Thirteen

*D*uring one of my visits with Bea she suggested I try to do automatic writing, just to see if I could. I should also add that Bea indicated that I should always say a few words asking for protection from any negative sources. In other words, not to open the door to just anyone.

I tried the writing once or twice with no results but in October, 1993, I started feeling as though I should attempt this again. My birthday was approaching and I was feeling down (all special occasions such as birthdays and holidays are extremely difficult after the loss of a child) and I kept having an urge to try the writing again.

At first I tried writing the letters of the alphabet. (Someone I knew who was able to do this type of writing had told me this was what she had done when she first started. She said her pen would point to each letter she was to write.) I next tried just scribbling and let my hand move where it seemed to want to go. After many, many pages of this, some of the scribbling started to look like letters written over and over again. I then tried writing the alphabet, again nothing, but after writing it a second time letters appeared, slanting down the page in a shaky, almost illegible writing. It read, "Erin loves" followed by scribbling that looked like a row of "M"s, and several lines of unreadable marks.

I must point out that I was not sitting all day trying to do this. I would stand and attempt this at my island bar in the kitchen for only a few minutes at a time as I somehow sensed that it was very important that it not interfere with my daily routine, or to become an obsession. After the writings became more readable I could tell when it would work the instant I placed the pen or pencil to the paper. The writing never continued for more than a few minutes at a time and, as I stated before, I had a sense of "this shouldn't interfere with your daily responsibilities," and it has not.

I have edited these writings for clarity. Much of what was written is unreadable, or the words that are legible do not fit together to make a complete thought, although I have included some of these fragmented sentences or phrases.

On October 21, the day following my birthday, I felt literally exhausted. I have discovered in the past five years that I "hang in there" for holidays, birthdays, etc., but I always experience a terrible letdown the following day, and this day followed the usual pattern. I again attempted to do more writing and after a phrase that had some discernable words which did not fit together to form a complete thought this followed:

Sorry you had to go thru this pain MOM these months. You are better now, much better now. I love you. Today don't (go or do)...thing. Erin wants to be there with you today. Book will be success. Bring book to Bea [name written was Bea's actual name], likes....Taste the cake. Better [batter] is always good. [My birthday cake was sitting nearby on the counter. Erin loved to lick the bowl and beaters whenever I made a cake.] Erin loves Mom.

I was completely overwhelmed. Could this really be happening or was it all my own doing? Thoroughly convinced for some time of Erin's continuing existence, I still was astonished to have any type of communication directly from her. This was not what I expected when I first attempted to do this. I had expected more of a generic type of writing, if it was possible to do it at all. There is no way to verbalize my emotions as these writings continued. Again I must point out that the feeling I had was that I should not let this become an obsession. It seemed to be very important that I keep it in balance with the rest of the happenings in my life. I cannot explain how I knew this, it was just a very strong feeling that I could not ignore. Intuition is the best word I can think of to use as an explanation.

When the following came through I was even more dumbfounded than before. Irena Thatch is Ron's grandmother and she and her husband, Irvin, raised Ron. He called them Mom and Dad. She had not known of Erin's death when she died in 1992 at age 93. When I wrote the word Irena, I had no idea what I had written. The letter "I" was written several times before the word Irena was completed:

> Irena Thatch. Couldn't know WRONG...Erin gone, could not tell...Mother...Ron love him a lot, love you too a lot, Liz too. [This was the only instance in these writings where Lizz was spelled "Liz." Irena did not know that Lizz had added an additional "z."] Ron, DAD here too. love him very...more later.

At this point I thought I was completely losing my mind. I told myself, "O.K., you must be doing this yourself" so I got a pen and paper, held the pen loosely in my hand and consciously wrote, "How are you, I am fine." This was followed by, and in different handwriting:

> Then why don't you believe me, I am here.

One of the next writings was as follows. I am not sure of the exact date as I did not start noting dates until a short time later:

This is Irvin Thatch. The book is good Helen. We're proud of you...Erin is with us. She is happy. His mom is here [this reference to "mom" had to mean Delorus, Ron's real mother]. She is O.K. Cole [a nickname used by Irvin for Ron's sister who is still living] is not happy. Helen—will you forgive us?

After about a week of doing these writings I decided to take a deep breath and show them to Ron. I was terrified that he would think I had gone completely insane and, to be quite honest, at this point I wasn't sure I hadn't. He quietly looked at them, then told me that it certainly didn't look like my handwriting, that part of it seemed to be similar to Erin's and that some looked like his grandmother's. Irena had written in a very shaky hand and the writings attributed to her are very similar. When I showed them to Lizz her comment was, "I shouldn't tell you this but it does look a little like Erin's writing." She also noted a similarity to her grandmother's handwriting, but she prefers to believe that all of this is coming from my sub-conscious.

The next time I decided to ask questions to see if I could actually communicate or if it was only a one-sided conversation.

I asked Erin if she was responsible for my friend not accompanying me to New York to see George Anderson, resulting in Ron making the trip with me:

Yes. Love you. No thanks necessary. Dad needed to go. Love him too. Hope he believes. Mom is O.K. now. I love you.

This was immediately followed by:

> Thatch. This is Irena. This is another time. How do I
> say I sorry. I love, love Ron. Butch [a nickname Ron's
> grandparents used for him], sorry. This is true.

The morning this was written I was missing Erin desperately. I stood in the shower sobbing and talking to her. I kept
repeating, "I love you, I miss you so much, I hope you know
how much I love you.":

> Mom love Erin. Do not be sad. Makes a difference....

Writing done November 17, 1993:

> [I asked, "Are you happy?"] Nobody is sad. ["Is it
> beautiful?"] Yes, beautiful. Maybe it is again today
> before [I do not understand the meaning of
> this]...Erin loves Mom and Dad very much.

This was written later the same day, soon after I received a
phone call from an acquaintance I will call Mary telling me
of her extraordinary writings and drawings (see following
chapter):

> Message to Mary is true. More later will Erin do.
> Much more to come. That is all for now.

Written November 20, the word Clombera appeared for the
first time. Clombera is not in the dictionary but clomb is an

archaic term meaning the past tense of climb. Era, of course, means period of time. Perhaps she is indicating that she has climbed to a new period in time, but that is just a guess on my part:

> Much to do in next life. How are you—Dad...I want to climb. Clombera. This is Christmas. Clombera. Person will come to you whenever you need to do something, teacher...much to do here.

This short message was written November 22:

> Climb I want to do.

November 24, again the word Clombera is mentioned:

> Clombera means place where there is peace to all who live there. Mom, I am here. It is important to have love in family now. Grandpa tunnel. Much to be done. I love all of family, all of family.

The following was written December 2. I had not attempted this for approximately a week because of a comment made by an acquaintance when I told him about the messages. He said that Erin had not been in the other dimension long enough to be able to accomplish this feat. It wasn't that he didn't believe in the possibility of this type of writing, he just didn't believe that she could do it. I must add that he did not know Erin:

Could be Mom run away. Clombera Christmas time.
I want to be much closer. That is what I want to do. I
want to do love...of only time is love. Time is love.
Time is love...our love is here. Our love is here. Mom.
Must go now. Love, love, love.

This was immediately followed by:

Irena here now. Love all of you. I miss you. I miss
you. How is Ron? Mother is O.K. now here, love her
very much. All today, more tomorrow. Love Erin,
much love, love. Irena Thatch. True is this. Must go.

I wrote this on December 4. This startled me even more than
the others, if that is possible, as I have never known or heard
of anyone named Marvin Morrison:

Marvin Morrison. Marvin...I like you too (sic) go to
Mable. Love her. Mrs. [this was followed by an obviously long name, some letters discernable but not
readable as a name]...order (?) to alive. [I asked, "Do
you want me to tell her you are alive?"] Yes. Mom
["Is she your mom?"] Yes...married now. I don't like
him...[The balance did not make sense, there were
the words "everyone," "tomorrow," "eleven."]

This came through to me on December 8:

Mom love you, love Dad. Must go to Lizz now. She
needs me now. Clombera. Peace here for me now...I
want to climb.

Written December 18.

> Mom love you...Mom love very much. Dad better now tomorrow. I love him too—more lonely—love him. Lonely when he goes to work, better now—before not always... Now between realm—learn only. I love you. I need to climb. I want to climb before I go to sleep again. I must do this...Much to learn here for me. Lizz love her. I love her...bye for now.

In mid-January, 1994 I received this communication:

> Mom, I love you. I'm here. Alive. Book O.K. now, will work. [This writing was interrupted because of the doorbell ringing. I had just completed a rewrite of a portion of the manuscript prior to this message.]

The following writings were done after I had completed the first draft on the final three chapters.

Written in early February, 1994:

> No more my time. Many lives before to...many lives. Many lives to do, many lives. Mom better now, much better now. Mom happy now. Yes, Mom happy now....

Three days later, from someone who remained nameless:

> Many lives we have, much work to do now. Much to

do next. ["What am I supposed to do next?"] Help others. ["How do I help others?"] Be you. ["Who is this?"] Friend, this is all.

I have a huge butterfly collection in a greenhouse window in my kitchen and for the past several years prior to these writings an interesting phenomenon has been taking place in relation to these butterflies. Hanging near this window are chimes consisting of three metal butterflies suspended at varied lengths. I have noticed that many times when I am thinking about Erin one or more of these butterflies will twist back and forth, more often than not it is only one that is moving. The day my sister Linda called to tell me about finding the butterfly necklace, one of the butterflies turned repeatedly. About a month prior to this writing, I realized that I hadn't seen them move since approximately the time I had started doing the automatic writing. The following is the last communication that I will include:

Erin is here today. Butterfly move, me do now. [I then looked up at my butterfly chimes and the center one (and only the center one) twisted back and forth several times. Nothing else hanging in or near the window moved. I was overwhelmed and overjoyed. Here was the proof I needed, the doubt has always been there, of course. Am I doing this myself or is it real? But I know I cannot make an object across the room move.] Mom happy now. Mom happy now. Much more to say. I alive...much to do now—much to do now...love, love, love. Time for me to go now. More to do another time...Mary good name. [This was written a short time after I had chosen Mary to be used for the name of the person who contributed to the following chapter.]

Chapter Fourteen

The following was written by an acquaintance whom I shall call Mary and deals with her decision to try to do automatic writing. In view of previous events, it was quite extraordinary that Mary would even attempt to do this. When I had first read the book about George Anderson, I mentioned to her that I would really like to talk to him. I can't remember exactly how Mary responded but I do recall that an invisible curtain had gone down between us. She was not receptive in the least to that idea.

When we made our plans to go to New York I did not tell Mary that we were going to see George, just that we were going there on vacation. She guessed, of course, the purpose of the so called vacation. When I talked to Mary upon our return there was still a certain coolness in her tone. I felt that she thought we had made a grave mistake. A short time later I sent Mary a copy of the tape I had made of our evening with George. It was six months later before she listened to it but after doing so she immediately called me, very excited, and from that day has been open to all possibilities:

> I hadn't made pies for a long time. But this afternoon seemed to be a good time. Making my usual mess, and tasting the pie dough from time to time, my thoughts drifted to Erin, I miss her everyday, but that afternoon was special. I found myself thinking about her as I made that pie and halfway wondering if she was helping me. It was a happy thought that perhaps she was.
>
> Several days later, I mentioned to Helen that my thoughts were with Erin during that pie making adventure, and she was appreciative of my thoughts, but there was also a sense of excitement in her voice because Erin "just loved pie dough."
>
> Later in the week, very tired after a days work, and not exactly concentrating on my task of writing a grocery list for the next day, my doodling habit directed me to the middle of my paper where I started to write the alphabet. My mind had wandered back to a conversation about automatic handwriting where the process was started by consciously writing the alphabet, and then an "automatic" process would take over. I was amazed anyone could do that. Well, I knew I could probably manage the alphabet. I wrote the letters and was about halfway through the second when the letters no longer were distinct. I kept going and my hand seemed to take on a mind of its own—no longer was I writing letters, but they

appeared more as scribbles. They were not random scribbles, however. Each mark was identical to the one before, with perfect spacing. Ten rows of marks, all the same—identical spacing. As I wrote, I noticed a tightening in my arm, and as I proceeded my right hand continued to tighten, and in a short time had completely changed position. I was now writing the marks with a hand that had completely turned into a left-handed position. I was astounded to feel the pressure in my arm and hand and to see those utterly nonsensical marks on that grocery list!

I was really curious by this time, and quite wide awake, as I knew something was happening that I had never experienced before. What I needed at the grocery store no longer seemed quite so important! I decided to start with a clean piece of paper. That piece was the first of hundreds.

Over the course of the next week, I sat down several times to see if I could repeat the experience. I was able to get into the "automatic" mode quite easily, each time feeling the pressure in my arm as my hand turned to the left-handed position.

I am reasonably patient by nature, and I needed to call on this patience as I continued to scribble wonderful marks on many, many sheets of paper— side-ways lines, up and down lines, and lots and lots of circles. Nothing really made sense to me at that time, but the marks all seemed to have a plan. They started and ended exactly the same. The space between them was exactly the same, and they went on paper after paper. My curiosity was piqued, and I felt if I kept going something might start to make sense.

The patience was rewarded. A pile of papers

later, the marks appeared more as letters, and then the letters went together to form a word—"Erin." I was elated, but not overly surprised. Although quite content with my accomplishment, I felt there might be more. Whenever I sat down, I would feel a real sense of childlike excitement. I felt as though I was unwrapping a gift with an unknown treasure inside. There was also a sense of fear involved, as this was not familiar territory I was dabbling in. Lack of control can be uncomfortable.

The second recognizable word I wrote was "butterfly." At this point, I was pretty amazed, because, since Erin's death, the butterfly has let itself be known in many wondrous ways. I, too, had experienced the appearance of the butterfly, and now I had confirmation of its significance.

After several days, the words appearing on the papers linked themselves together, giving more and more meaning to this "writing experience." The word "evil" often appeared, along with "Erin," "butterfly," "believe," and "tunnel." These phrases were written, "Erin evil ends" and "believe first and evil will end." Finally, it all came together. "BELIEVE IN THE BUTTERFLY AND EVIL WILL END" was the message written over and over again.

The next day, my hand seemed to not want to write letters or words. Instead, a drawing mode seemed to appear. I tried to relax and let my hand and pencil do what they wanted—big circles, little circles, scribbles up and down. I seemed to be reverting back to my initial attempts, and I was somewhat disappointed. However, as my scribbles suddenly turned into a recognizable picture of a butterfly, I was revived. I couldn't believe it! I kept drawing butterflies, and they always had a line extending away from them, meandering here and there, but almost always ending in a tightly drawn circle. I remembered having written the word "tunnel" many times earlier and it was at this point that I realized that the tightly drawn circles represented a tunnel.

I think whoever was guiding my writing efforts decided I was better suited for drawing because from that point on I drew. [H.F.—Actually what Mary told me was that she had the feeling it was being indicated, "What do we have to do, draw you a picture?"] Occasionally, a word or phrase would be thrown in, but not often. Human and angel forms appeared along with the butterfly and a multitude of tunnels. At one point, often repeated later, the human form was connected by line to the butterfly, and from the butterfly to the tunnel. At the bottom of one of these pages was written, "Erin found tunnel."

Human transformation takes place through the spiritual belief of the butterfly was my interpretation. If we believe in the butterfly as a symbol of transformation, it will lead us through not one, but many spiritual tunnels. If the butterfly, or a spiritual belief, is not present in this process, "evil" is able to enter the tunnels. All of this seemed consistent with the original message, "BELIEVE IN THE BUTTERFLY AND EVIL WILL END."

I don't understand the significance or the meaning of all of this experience at this point in time. But I do believe I have been given an opening for further understanding, and that Erin will be there enjoying every minute!

As I typed this chapter, I arrived at another possible interpretation of these drawings, or an extension of Mary's interpretation.

The butterfly signifies a transformation from one life to another: a symbol of everlasting life. In a sense, we come full circle back to where we originated, the tunnel being the connection between the two dimensions. If this concept was widely accepted as truth, humans would perhaps be less apt to do unkind, evil deeds to one another. If our memory survives the death of our bodies, and from our experiences of the past five years it certainly seems to do so, the memory of those we have been linked to in this life also survives. This means we will ultimately come face to face with those whom may have been harmed by our actions. In many of the near death experiences related in recent books, there seems to be a life review after a person goes through the tunnel. No judgement is made, but the consequences of your actions, and inactions, are made clear; you become aware of the connection between what you have done, or neglected to do, and other souls, and perhaps to the world as a whole. If this interpretation is correct, then what we do to others, and to this beautiful planet, will live on forever with us into what we call eternity.

Another thought is that if you believe in what the butterfly represents the concept of evil can no longer exist, because in achieving this level of belief you have grown so much spiritually that you can no longer possibly conceive of hurting another living being.

Goodbye

The following is a song recorded by Night Ranger and chosen by Lizz to be played at the "Celebration of Erin's Life" as a gift to Ron and me. It seemed the only appropriate ending to this, Erin's book:

> As the sun hides his head
> For another night's rest
> And the wind sings
> His same old song
> And you on the edge
> Never close, never far
> Always there when I needed a friend
>> Yet it's hard living life
>> On this memory-go-round
>> Always up, always down
>> Spinning round and round
>> And all this could be
>> Just a dream so it seems
>> I was never much good at goodbye
> There once was a time
> Never far from my mind
> On the beach, on the 4th of July
> I remember the sand

How you held out your hand
And we touched for what seemed a lifetime
Now it's hard
Leaving all this behind me now
Like a schoolboy so lost
Never found until now
    And all this could be
    Just a dream so it seems
    I was never much good at goodbye
    Yet it's hard
    Living life on this memory-go-round
    Always up, always down
    Turning round and round
    And all this could be
    Just a dream so it seems
    I was never much good at goodbye.

    Goodbye.

       As ever, with love,

      Erin Lynn Fisher

Epilogue

*E*rin Fisher, my daughter, my friend. What a legacy she has left behind. She had to condense a lifetime into too few years but what a successful lifetime it was. Her love of life just bubbled from her. She had this wonderful knack of making the most ordinary happening exciting, and, believe me, she never held back in showing this excitement. She passionately cared for people. In the words of one of her cousins after a visit to us, "Erin makes everyone feel important." What a tremendous gift.

She could also make you feel her wrath in a way not easily forgotten, she was no polly-anna by any means, and "Moms" many times was the subject of this wrath. And often as not "Moms" learned something as a result. But Erin was also as quick to say, "I'm sorry" as she was to anger. She, of course, didn't like everyone, or everyone like her, but I would almost guarantee no one who met her would forget her. Those beautiful, huge brown eyes, whether sparkling with excitement or sparking with anger, were not easily forgotten.

She made an impact on all who knew her. During that last tragic week we had nurses tell us their lives would never be the same after meeting Erin, and one who said this had never seen her in a conscious state. The following is an excerpt from a letter written by her doctor, Maxine Nichols:

> Rarely is a letter as difficult to compose as this one. Erin had a profound effect on everyone she touched and the last week of her life left many people changed for the rest of their lives.

Erin liked to laugh but she also had a very serious side and was very concerned about the environment and the social ills which plague society today, particularly the problem of the homeless. I remember one instance when she went to San Francisco by herself and came back with this wonderful story that she told with eyes just dancing.

A homeless man had asked her for money and she decided to give him a few dollars. Now keep in mind the image of this young woman and imagine her getting right in front of him, shaking her finger in his face and telling him he had to promise to buy food, not booze. This drew quite a crowd of onlookers whom I'm sure enjoyed it immensely because she had such an expressive face and manner. She said as she walked down the street she could hear him shouting, "Buy food, no booze, buy food, no booze." And perhaps he did just that, but, if not, he at least had contact for a few moments with someone who truly cared.

In writing this book I have gone out on a limb, and with the addition of the last three chapters I feel I have just been handed a saw. If I did not believe 100% in all that has transpired since Erin's death, believe me, I would not be standing out on this limb for the entire world to scrutinize, and I will be scrutinized, of that I have no doubt. But I also am quite aware that all of this must be shared. The feeling of a hand in the middle of the back pushing me to do so is always with me.

The compiling of this book has not been easy for me but a task I knew had to be undertaken. I have relived every moment of her illness with this writing and many tears have been shed in the process. It has also been frightening to realize that with the publishing of *From Erin with Love* we are no longer the private people we have always been. But if this book helps even one person in dealing with grief or a terminal illness, then the loss of privacy is a small price to pay.

I have a memory of sitting on my couch in October, 1990, and knowing I had to make a choice, do I sink or swim? I made the choice to swim, and from that day forward I began to heal, very slowly and very painfully, but to heal. I made the decision that I wanted to live my life in such a way that Erin would be proud of me. Seeing how she handled her illness with such courage and fierce determination taught me so very much. I have drawn from this knowledge to help come out of the darkness that one is plunged into after losing a child.

I have read that up to 70% of bereaved parents sense the presence or even see their child after death. This is quickly put down as unacceptable by our society, as not possible. But remember, at one point in time the earth was perceived as flat. Any opinion to the contrary was considered heresy. Even the idea of doctors doing something as important as washing their hands before delivering a baby was once considered unnecessary. If you couldn't see germs then obviously they didn't exist, and this way of thinking even continued for many years after germs and bacteria were proven to exist. As a result countless numbers of women died unnecessarily.

The idea of a man walking on the moon was once considered only the wild imagination of science fiction writers but that, too, became a reality. Is reality only what we perceive with our eyes, or with a powerful microscope, or does reality have boundless limits? Reality to those living in the 1500s was certainly different than it is to us today, but does that mean that much of what we deem real today didn't exist then? No, of course not. We were just unaware.

This beautiful planet on which we live is a miracle in itself. The concept of life after death is another miracle, a reality we just have yet to prove conclusively. *Closer to the Light* by Dr. Melvin Morse is a good example of our ever increasing awareness of this other dimension. This book deals with near death experiences of children and certainly helps to confirm much of what we have experienced.

Erin attacked life head-on and the most lasting tribute to her is for all of us to embrace life to its fullest. Reach out and touch someone with love and caring, take the time to see the beauty of the earth and work to save it. Take the time to care. Isn't that what life is all about? And from time to time think of this gift from Erin, the knowledge of life after death, and reflect upon what this really means.

We obviously take no possessions with us when we leave this earth but if we can accept the premise of this book and what we have learned from Erin, it points to our ability to take our "self" and our capacity to love. We certainly don't take our bodies, they are just the vehicles for the soul, the part of us that I believe survives death. We are all driving these different colored vehicles on our journey, on this roller coaster ride we call life. We are all of one race, the race known as humanity, and we are all connected as a whole.

Love, caring, and the art of giving to others is the secret of life Erin discovered at such an early age. She was a person who would go to great lengths to keep a promise, especially a promise made to her sister, and she has, despite overwhelmingly insurmountable odds, kept that promise. May we all learn from her example, and practice what we have learned:

> And share the message from above
> The business of life is simply to love.

Author's Note:

*D*uring the course of writing this book, many people have shared experiences which validate that the events noted in *From Erin with Love* are not unique. The author invites readers to send similar happenings to be used for possible inclusion in a future book. Credit will be given for all contributions used, or they will be included anonymously if that is preferred. Please mail to:

Helen M. Fisher

c/o Swallowtail Publishing

P.O. Box 2037

San Ramon, CA 94583

GRIFFIN PRINTING
C. Penny Hancock
4141 N. Freeway Blvd.
Sacramento, CA 95834
(800) 448-3511 • (916) 649-3511
FAX (916) 649-0238

Cover & Interior Design
Lightbourne Images
300 Sheridan St., Ashland, OR 97520
(503) 488-3060 • FAX (503) 482-1730

Order Form

Telephone Orders: (510) 803-0912
FAX Orders: (500) 674-8703 • (510) 803-4098
Postal Orders: Swallowtail Publishing
P.O. Box 2037, San Ramon, CA 94583

Name: _____

Address: _____

City: _____ State:___ Zip: _____

Telephone: (___)_____

Please send ___copies @ $12.95 ea. $____.__

Shipping:

Book Rate: $2.00 for first

book and 75 cents each additional book.

First Class: $3.50 per book $____.__

Sales Tax: CA residents add $1.07

                              per book $____.__

                              Total: $____.__

Paid by: Check___

Credit Card:___   Visa___   MasterCard___

Name on card:_____

Number on card:_____Exp. Date___